Mindset Matters

By Dr. Shamarah J. Hutchins
TheMindologist

Copyright © 2025

ISBN: 978-1-7352735-8-7 (Print)
ISBN: 978-1-7352735-9-4 (Digital)

All rights reserved. No part of this book may be reproduced or utilized in any form or by any means, electronic or mechanical, including photocopying, recording, or by any information storage or retrieval systems, without permission in writing from the publisher, except for the use of brief quotations in a book reviews.

PART I

Your mindset sets the thermostat for your life.

Adjust it, and everything shifts.

Chapter 1
Introduction: Why Mindset Matters

Welcome to Mindset Matters. I'm Dr. Shamarah J. Hutchins, but many people know me as TheMindologist — a title I carry with pride because it reflects my life's work and passion for understanding how the mind shapes every part of our existence. My journey to becoming TheMindologist wasn't easy, but it was intentional. Through my personal experiences, my work in mental health, and my deep understanding of emotional regulation and human behavior, I've learned one essential truth: your mindset is the foundation of everything you experience in life.

You may have heard phrases like "Change your mindset, change your life" — but how often have you actually been shown how to do that? That's exactly what this book is about. I'm not just here to give you motivational quotes or quick fixes. I want to walk with you through the process of transforming your thinking at the core level, so that the shifts you experience become permanent, not just temporary highs.

Why Mindset Matters

Your mindset is the lens through which you experience the world. It's the filter that shapes your decisions, your reactions, and even how you define success and happiness. If that lens is fogged by fear, doubt, or negative self-talk, it distorts everything — your goals, your relationships, and even your self-worth.

This book will help you understand:

- Why your current mindset might be holding you back.
- How to shift from a fixed mindset to a growth mindset.
- How to identify and eliminate self-limiting beliefs.
- How to reframe setbacks and failures as opportunities for growth.
- How to regulate your emotions so that you stay grounded even when life challenges you.

What You'll Gain from This Book

By the time you finish Mindset Matters, you'll have more than just knowledge, you'll have a blueprint for a new way of living. This isn't about becoming someone you're not; it's about unlocking the version of yourself that already exists beneath the doubt and mental clutter. You'll learn how to:

Develop emotional resilience and self-confidence.

Cultivate habits that align with your values and goals.

Face challenges with clarity and strength.

Create a mindset that not only supports your success but also sustains it.

This book is a shift in how you experience your life. Whether you're looking to grow personally, professionally, or both, the principles in Mindset Matters will equip you with the tools to create lasting change.

So, are you ready? Let's get started…….. because your mindset matters.

A renewed mind leads to a rerouted destiny.

Chapter 2:
The Power of Thought – How Your Mind Shapes Your Reality

In the introduction, we explored why mindset matters — how the way you think influences the way you experience life. Now, we're going to take that idea deeper by focusing on the mechanics of thought itself. If mindset is the foundation, your thoughts are the building blocks. The quality of your thoughts determines the quality of your mindset, and ultimately, the quality of your life.

But here's the truth most people overlook: your thoughts aren't just reactions to the world — they are the architects of it. The way you think actively shapes your reality. Every success or setback, every relationship, every opportunity — they all start in the mind. And until you learn to master your thoughts, you'll struggle to master your life.

How Thoughts Become Reality

Have you ever noticed how two people can experience the exact same situation but have completely different takeaways?

Imagine two people walking into a job interview. Both are equally qualified and prepared. But Person A thinks, "I'm probably not going to get this job. I always mess these things up." Person B thinks, "I've prepared for this. I'm confident and capable."

Even though their skill sets are equal, their thoughts are not. Person A will walk into that interview hesitant, guarded, and insecure — and the interviewer will likely sense it. Person B will walk in with open body language, speak with confidence, and likely leave a stronger impression. The outcome? Person B lands the job while Person A reinforces their belief that they aren't good enough — even though the truth is they were equally capable.

The thoughts you have create the emotional state you carry into every situation. And that emotional state shapes how you respond to opportunities, challenges, and setbacks.

The Thought-Emotion-Behavior Loop

Your thoughts create a domino effect that influences how you feel and, in turn, how you act. This is called the Thought-Emotion-Behavior Loop:

- Thought → What you tell yourself about a situation.
- Emotion → The feeling that results from that thought (fear, confidence, doubt, motivation).
- Behavior → How you respond based on that emotion.

Let's break this down with an example:

Thought: "I'm not good at public speaking."

Emotion: Anxiety, fear of embarrassment.

Behavior: Avoiding opportunities to speak, stumbling through presentations when forced to do them.

Outcome: Poor performance reinforces the original belief of "I'm not good at this."

Now let's flip the script:

Thought: "I'm prepared, and even if I stumble, I'll recover."

Emotion: Confidence and calm.

Behavior: Speaking with clarity and ease.

Outcome: Improved performance reinforces confidence.

See how the shift starts at the thought level? You can't expect to feel confident or act decisively if your thoughts are undermining you at the core.

Your Brain on Autopilot: The Power of Conditioning

Here's the tricky part — most of your thoughts are happening automatically, beneath the surface of your awareness. Studies show that up to 95% of your thoughts are repetitive and driven by subconscious programming. This means that your thoughts are usually reflecting past conditioning rather than conscious choice.

For example, if you grew up hearing things like:

- "Money doesn't grow on trees."
- "Relationships are hard work."
- "You're not smart enough to do that."

...those thoughts become mental shortcuts that shape your behavior. You might avoid financial risks, sabotage relationships, or hold yourself back from career opportunities — not because you aren't capable, but because your subconscious mind is running an outdated program.

Reframing: How to Take Back Control of Your Thoughts

To reshape your reality, you have to start by interrupting negative or limiting thoughts before they take root. This is where reframing comes in — consciously shifting the way you interpret situations.

Example of Reframing:

❌ "I can't do this."
✅ "I'm figuring this out — and every step is making me better."
❌ "I always fail at this."
✅ "I'm learning from every attempt, and it's making me stronger."

Reframing isn't about lying to yourself. It's about telling yourself a more helpful and empowering truth. When you replace limiting thoughts with empowering ones, you shift your emotional state — and that shift changes how you show up in the world.

The Science Behind It: Neuroplasticity

Your brain isn't fixed — it's constantly rewiring itself based on how you think and behave. This is called neuroplasticity — the brain's ability to form new neural connections.

When you repeat a thought (whether positive or negative), you strengthen the neural pathway connected to it. If you tell yourself over and over, "I'm not good enough," that pathway gets stronger, and your brain starts defaulting to that thought automatically.

But here's the good news: You can weaken old pathways and build new ones.

- Every time you catch yourself thinking a negative thought and consciously reframe it, you weaken the old pathway.
- Every time you repeat a new, empowering thought, you strengthen a new pathway.
- Over time, your brain starts defaulting to the new thought automatically — which means your mindset shifts at the core level.

Shifting From a Fixed to a Growth Mindset

Dr. Carol Dweck's research on fixed and growth mindsets provides a powerful framework for how this works.

- A fixed mindset believes that your abilities and traits are set in stone. (e.g., "I'm just not good at math.")
- A growth mindset believes that your abilities can develop with effort and practice. (e.g., "I can get better at math with practice.")

Shifting to a growth mindset requires training your brain to see effort and failure as part of the learning process rather than proof that you aren't good enough.

Example:

- Fixed Mindset → "I failed the test, so I'm just bad at this."
- Growth Mindset → "I didn't do well this time, but I understand where I went wrong. I can improve."

Practical Exercises to Train Your Thoughts

Here are two simple but powerful exercises to help you start rewiring your thoughts:

1. Thought Catching

- Spend 5 minutes each morning writing down any negative or limiting thoughts that come to mind.
- Once you have the list, challenge each thought:
    - Is this true?
    - Is this helpful?
    - What's a more empowering way to frame this?

2. Affirmation Repetition

- Write down 5 empowering thoughts related to your goals (e.g., "I am confident and capable.").
- Repeat them out loud every morning for 30 days.
- Visualize yourself living out those thoughts while you say them.

Mastering Your Thoughts = Mastering Your Reality

Your mind is your most powerful tool — but it can also be your greatest enemy if you leave it unchecked. When you become aware of your thoughts and learn to shift them, you take control over your life.

This chapter laid the foundation for recognizing and reframing your thoughts. In the next chapter, we'll dive deeper into the difference between a fixed mindset and a growth mindset — and how choosing a growth mindset can unlock levels of success and fulfillment you didn't think were possible.

Because when you change your thoughts, you change your reality.

Chapter 3: Breaking Mental Barriers — Overcoming Fear and Doubt

We've already uncovered how your thoughts shape your reality and influence your emotional state and behavior. Now, it's time to address two of the most common and destructive mental barriers that can block your progress: fear and self-doubt. Understanding how these barriers operate — and learning how to overcome them — is essential for sustaining confidence and momentum.

Fear and doubt are hardwired into the human brain for survival. Thousands of years ago, these emotions protected us from real threats like predators and environmental dangers. But in the modern world, these same instincts often misfire — holding you back from taking chances, chasing opportunities, and reaching your full potential.

If you've ever hesitated to take action because you were afraid of failing, being judged, or not being good enough — you've experienced this firsthand. But the good news is that fear and doubt are not fixed traits. They are conditioned responses — which means they can be rewired and overcome.

Understanding Fear and Doubt

Let's define what we're really dealing with:

Fear = Emotional Response to Perceived Threat

- Fear is triggered when your brain senses danger — whether real or imagined.
- Fear creates physical and mental responses: racing heart, tense muscles, overthinking, and avoidance.

Doubt = Lack of Confidence in Yourself or Your Abilities

- Doubt is the inner voice that says, "You're not good enough," or "What if you fail?"
- Doubt stems from internalized past failures, criticism, or negative experiences.

Fear and doubt often work together. Fear creates hesitation; doubt convinces you that you're not capable. This cycle becomes a self-fulfilling prophecy — because when you hesitate and hold back, you reinforce the belief that you aren't capable or that things will go wrong.

How Fear and Doubt Develop

Fear and doubt don't come from nowhere — they are learned behaviors, shaped by experience and reinforced by repetition.

1. Early Conditioning

Many of your mental barriers were formed in childhood. If you were criticized for making mistakes or felt pressure to be perfect, you might have developed the belief that failure = weakness.

Example:

- If you were laughed at during a school presentation, you might have formed the belief that you're bad at public speaking — even though one bad experience doesn't define your ability.

2. Social and Cultural Programming

Society often reinforces fear and doubt by setting unrealistic standards for success and perfection.

- The fear of judgment from others creates a cycle of avoidance.
- Social media amplifies this by constantly showing curated, polished versions of success — making it easy to feel like you're falling behind.

Example:

- You see someone posting about their business success online. Instead of feeling inspired, you feel inadequate and start thinking, "I'll never be able to do that."

3. Negative Self-Talk

Fear and doubt thrive when you repeat negative thoughts to yourself:

- "I'm not smart enough."
- "What if I mess up?"
- "I'm not qualified for this."

The brain doesn't distinguish between truth and repeated suggestion — if you tell yourself you're not capable enough, your mind will believe it and act accordingly.

The Fear-Doubt Loop

Just like the Thought-Emotion-Behavior Loop we explored earlier, fear and doubt create their own destructive cycle:

- Thought: "I'm probably going to fail."
- Emotion: Fear, anxiety, hesitation.
- Behavior: Avoidance or low-effort attempt.
- Outcome: Failure or lack of progress reinforces the belief that you're not capable.

This cycle is why many people stay stuck in the same patterns for years — fear creates hesitation, doubt convinces you to play small, and the lack of success reinforces the belief that you're not capable.

How to Break the Cycle of Fear and Doubt

Breaking mental barriers requires disrupting this pattern at the source — your thoughts. Here's how to shift from a fear-driven mindset to a confidence-based one:

1. Reframe Fear as a Signal of Growth

Fear is not always a sign of danger — often, it's a signal that you're stepping outside of your comfort zone.

- If you're never afraid, you're probably not growing.
- Fear shows up when you're challenging yourself — which means you're on the edge of a breakthrough.

Example:

Instead of thinking, "I'm scared to start this business because I might fail," try:

- "This fear means I'm about to grow. I'm stepping into something new — and that's a good thing."

2. Develop a Courage Ritual

Confidence isn't the absence of fear — it's the ability to take action in spite of fear. Create a ritual to center yourself when fear arises.

Example:

- Take 3 deep breaths.
- Repeat a positive affirmation ("I am prepared. I am capable.").
- Take the smallest next step.

Even small steps teach your brain that fear doesn't control you — and the more you face fear, the less power it holds over you.

3. Stop Asking "What If?" — Start Asking "What's the Worst That Can Happen?"

Fear thrives on uncertainty. Your mind creates exaggerated stories about what might go wrong.

- Instead of spiraling into "What if I fail?" — ask yourself, "What's the worst that can actually happen?"
- When you name the fear, it loses power.
- You'll realize that even the worst-case scenario is usually manageable — and not life-ending.

Example:

Fear: "What if I embarrass myself in this presentation?"

Reframe: "The worst that can happen is I stumble. But I can recover, and I'll get better next time."

4. Challenge Doubt with Evidence

Doubt is a liar. It tells you that you aren't capable — but you have evidence to prove otherwise.

- Write down 5 times you succeeded or overcame a challenge in the past.
- When doubt creeps in, remind yourself of those victories.
- Build on that evidence — if you succeeded before, you can succeed again.

Example:

Doubt: "I'm not good at interviews."

Counter: "I've nailed interviews before. I know how to prepare and stay calm. I've done it before — I can do it again."

5. Build Confidence Through Small Wins

You don't overcome fear and doubt through massive leaps — you do it through small, consistent wins.

- Set small, achievable goals.
- Celebrate progress — not perfection.
- Each small win reinforces the belief that you are capable.

Example:

- If you're afraid of public speaking, start by talking in small groups.
- Gradually work up to larger audiences.
- Each successful attempt builds confidence.

Practical Exercises to Overcome Fear and Doubt

1. The Fear Ladder

    - Write down something you fear doing.
    - Break it down into smaller steps — from least scary to most scary.
    - Start with the smallest step and build upward.

Example:

   - Fear = Public Speaking
       - Step 1 = Speaking in front of close friends
       - Step 2 = Speaking in a small group at work
       - Step 3 = Speaking at a large meeting

2. Confidence Anchoring

    - Think of a time when you succeeded or overcame a challenge.
    - Close your eyes and mentally recreate that moment — see it, feel it.
    - When fear creeps in, recall that moment to remind yourself that you're capable.

Fear and Doubt Are Not Your Enemy

Fear and doubt are natural — but they don't have to control you. When you learn to face fear directly and challenge doubt with truth, you take away their power.

Success isn't about being fearless — it's about learning how to act even when fear is present. Confidence comes from proving to yourself that you can handle challenges, and that proof comes from action.

In the next chapter, we'll explore the key to sustaining this momentum: developing emotional regulation so you stay grounded even when fear and doubt try to creep back in.

Because you don't have to be fearless — you just have to be brave enough to try.

Chapter 4: Self-Awareness — Understanding Your Inner Voice

Previously, we explored how fear and doubt can prevent you from stepping into your potential — and how to break free from that cycle. But to truly master your mindset, you need to dig deeper. Fear and doubt don't arise randomly; they stem from internal patterns and hidden beliefs that often operate beneath the surface.

That place is your inner voice — the constant mental dialogue running in the background of your mind. It's the voice that narrates your experiences, assigns meaning to events, and ultimately shapes how you see yourself and the world.

Some people's inner voice is a supportive coach, encouraging them to take risks and trust their instincts. For others, it's a harsh critic — reminding them of every failure, mistake, and shortcoming.

The difference between success and struggle isn't just your ability or luck — it's how your inner voice speaks to you. If you've ever wondered why you sabotage your progress or struggle to maintain confidence even after success, the answer lies in how you relate to your inner voice.

In this chapter, we'll explore how to identify your inner voice, recognize whether it's working for or against you, and learn how to shift it from a source of self-criticism to a source of empowerment.

What Is the Inner Voice?

Your inner voice is essentially the mental commentary that shapes how you interpret and respond to life.

It's not necessarily a literal "voice" — it's the collection of thoughts, beliefs, and mental patterns that run automatically in your mind.

This internal dialogue starts forming early in life and is influenced by:

- Parental feedback ("You're so smart!" vs. "Why can't you get this right?")
- School experiences ("You're a leader." vs. "You'll never be good at math.")
- Peer relationships ("You're so funny!" vs. "Nobody likes you.")
- Cultural messaging ("You have to be thin to be beautiful.")

Over time, these messages become part of your subconscious programming — and they shape how you see yourself and the world.

The Two Sides of the Inner Voice

Everyone has two versions of their inner voice:

- The Inner Coach
    - Encouraging and motivating
    - Focuses on strengths and potential
    - Helps you recover from setbacks
    - Speaks with kindness and understanding

Example:

"You didn't get the job, but you're learning. Keep going — you'll land the right one soon."

- The Inner Critic
    - Negative and judgmental
    - Focuses on flaws and limitations
    - Harsh and unforgiving
    - Promotes fear and avoidance

Example:

"You didn't get the job because you're not good enough. Why bother trying again?"

The problem is that for most people, the Inner Critic is louder than the Inner Coach — especially when you've experienced failure, criticism, or rejection.

Where Your Inner Voice Comes From

Your inner voice isn't something you were born with — it was shaped over time by life experiences and the environment you grew up in.

1. Parental and Caregiver Influence

- If your parents were critical or perfectionistic, you might have internalized that voice as your own.
- If you were praised for effort rather than results, you likely developed a more supportive inner voice.

2. Social and Cultural Messages

- Society promotes achievement, beauty, and success — which can lead to self-criticism when you feel you aren't measuring up.
- Media and social media create unrealistic standards — leading your inner critic to tell you that you aren't good enough.

3. Personal Failures and Successes

- If you experienced early success, you might have developed a confident inner voice.
- If you experienced repeated setbacks, your inner voice might default to doubt and fear.

How Your Inner Voice Shapes Your Behavior

Your inner voice is more than just mental noise — it directly affects your emotional state and actions.

- The Inner Voice Cycle
    - Inner Thought: "You're not good at this."
    - Emotional Response: Anxiety and hesitation.

- Behavior: You hold back or give up.
- Outcome: Failure or missed opportunity reinforces the original thought.

Example:

- Thought: "I'm terrible at social situations."
- Emotion: Anxiety and discomfort.
- Behavior: Avoids social situations.
- Outcome: Isolation reinforces the belief that you're bad at connecting with others.

Becoming Aware of Your Inner Voice

You can't change your inner dialogue if you aren't aware of it. The first step is to observe how your inner voice speaks to you throughout the day.

Exercise: Inner Voice Tracking

1. Spend one day noticing the thoughts that come up when you:
   - Face a challenge
   - Make a mistake
   - Receive praise or criticism
2. Write down what your inner voice says in these moments.
3. At the end of the day, review the list. Ask yourself:
   - Is this thought true?
   - Is it helpful or harmful?
   - Where might this thought have come from?

Example:

- Thought: "I'll probably mess this up."
- Truth: No evidence that you'll mess up.
- Source: Fear from a past experience.

How to Change Your Inner Voice

Once you've identified the patterns of your inner dialogue, you can begin to shift them. Here's how:

1. Name the Critic

Give your inner critic a name or identity — this helps separate it from your true self.

- "Oh, that's just 'Doubtful Dave' talking again."
- By naming it, you create emotional distance — which makes it easier to ignore.

2. Replace Judgment with Curiosity

Instead of judging yourself when you make a mistake, get curious:

- "Why did that happen?"
- "What can I learn from this?"
- "How can I improve next time?"

Example:

Critic: "You're terrible at this."

Curiosity: "What specifically didn't work — and how can I adjust?"

3. Reframe Negative Thoughts

Once you identify a negative thought, challenge and reframe it:

- ❌ "I'll never get this right."
- ✅ "I didn't get it right this time, but I'm learning and improving."

4. Build Evidence Against Your Critic

Your critic thrives on self-doubt — so create proof that you're capable.

- Keep a "Wins List" of achievements (big and small).
- When your critic says, "You're not good at this," remind yourself of past successes.

5. Strengthen the Inner Coach

Your inner coach needs intentional training.

- Create a list of positive affirmations.
- Speak to yourself the way you would speak to a close friend.
- Celebrate small wins to reinforce positive self-talk.

Example:

- "I handled that situation well."
- "I showed up and gave my best."
- "I'm learning, and that's enough."

Practical Exercise: Positive Affirmation Mirror Work

- Stand in front of a mirror every morning.
- Look yourself in the eyes and say three positive affirmations out loud.
- Do this consistently to strengthen the voice of the Inner Coach.

Example:

- "I am enough."
- "I am capable."

- "I trust myself."

You Are Not Your Thoughts

Your inner voice is not your identity — it's a learned habit. And like any habit, it can be reshaped.

By learning to observe your inner dialogue, question your critic, and strengthen your inner coach, you take control of the most powerful tool you have — your mind.

In the next chapter, we'll dive into one of the most powerful mindset shifts of all — moving from a fixed mindset to a growth mindset — and how this shift will unlock new levels of success and fulfillment.

Because when you change your inner voice, you change your entire life.

Recap of Part 1: Foundation of the Mindset Shift

Congratulations! You've made it through Part 1 of Mindset Matters — and that's no small feat. If you've followed along so far, you've already laid the foundation for a powerful mindset shift.

Part 1 was all about understanding the roots of your mindset — how your thoughts, emotions, and inner dialogue shape your reality. It provided you with the tools to recognize the mental patterns that might be holding you back and gave you strategies to start reshaping them.

Before we step into Part 2: Cultivating a Growth Mindset, let's pull everything together and review the core takeaways from Part 1. This will ensure you're fully equipped to build on this foundation moving forward.

Key Takeaways from Part 1

- **Why Mindset Matters (Introduction)**

- Your mindset is the lens through which you experience life.
- A negative or limited mindset creates emotional and behavioral patterns that hold you back.
- A positive, empowered mindset opens up new possibilities for growth and success.
- You have the power to shift your mindset — and this book is your guide to doing just that.

- **The Power of Thought (Chapter 2)**
    - Your thoughts are not passive — they are the foundation of your reality.
    - Thoughts → Emotions → Behavior → Outcomes → Reinforcement
    - Negative thought cycles reinforce limiting beliefs and keep you stuck.
    - You can challenge and reframe negative thoughts to break this cycle.

Example:

- Thought: "I'm terrible at public speaking."
- Reframed Thought: "I can improve my speaking skills through practice."

- **Breaking Mental Barriers (Chapter 3)**
    - Fear and doubt are survival instincts — but they are not truth.
    - Fear signals growth — not failure.
    - Taking action despite fear builds confidence and weakens doubt.

- Confidence comes from small, repeated wins — not perfection.

Example:

- Fear: "What if I fail?"
- Reframe: "Failure is part of growth — I can learn from it."

- **Self-Awareness and Inner Voice (Chapter 4)**
    - Your inner voice is the narrator of your life.
    - The inner critic undermines confidence; the inner coach builds it.
    - You can shift from self-criticism to self-support through reframing.
    - Self-awareness is the first step to rewiring your mindset.

Example:

- Inner Critic: "You're not good enough."
- Inner Coach: "You are learning and improving every day."

How These Pieces Fit Together

Mindset work isn't about fixing a single problem — it's about rewiring the whole system:

- First, you have to become aware of your thoughts.
- Then, you need to challenge and reframe those thoughts.
- Once you shift the thought, you'll shift the emotional state attached to it.

- That new emotional state will drive different behavior.
- The new behavior will create new outcomes — which will reinforce the new belief.

Old Pattern:

- Thought → "I'm not good at this."
- Emotion → Fear and hesitation
- Behavior → Avoidance or low effort
- Outcome → Failure reinforces doubt

New Pattern:

- Thought → "I'm improving with practice."
- Emotion → Confidence and motivation
- Behavior → Consistent effort and action
- Outcome → Success reinforces belief

This is the core cycle of mindset change — and now you know how to control it.

Home Exercise: The Thought Awareness Challenge

To solidify what you've learned in Part 1, here's an exercise you can do at home — either on your own or with a partner or group. This will help you strengthen self-awareness and practice reframing in real time.

Step 1: Set a Timer (10–15 Minutes)

Sit down in a quiet place, set a timer, and grab a notebook or journal.

Step 2: Thought Catching

Write down the first five thoughts that come to mind when you think about a goal, challenge, or opportunity in your life. Be honest — even if the thoughts are negative or uncomfortable.

- Example:
    - "I'm not good enough to get promoted."
    - "What if I mess up?"
    - "I don't know enough yet."
    - "Other people are better than me."
    - "I'll probably fail."

Step 3: Label Each Thought

Next to each thought, label it as:

- Helpful → Thought supports growth and confidence.
- Harmful → Thought promotes fear, doubt, or hesitation.

- Example:
    - "I'm not good enough to get promoted." → Harmful
    - "What if I mess up?" → Harmful
    - "I don't know enough yet." → Neutral
    - "Other people are better than me." → Harmful
    - "I'll probably fail." → Harmful

Step 4: Challenge the Harmful Thoughts

For every harmful thought, ask yourself:

- Is this true?
- Is there evidence to support this thought?
- What would a supportive version of this thought sound like?

- Example:
    - Harmful Thought: "I'm not good enough to get promoted."

- Is it true? → No.
- Evidence? → I've done well in my role and received positive feedback.
- Reframed Thought → "I'm prepared for the next step — I've put in the work."

Step 5: Rewrite the Narrative

Now rewrite the list with reframed thoughts for each harmful one:

- Example:
    - "I'm not good enough to get promoted." → "I've earned this opportunity through hard work."
    - "What if I mess up?" → "I might mess up — and I'll adjust and improve."
    - "I don't know enough yet." → "I'm learning every day."
    - "Other people are better than me." → "My skills and strengths are valuable."
    - "I'll probably fail." → "I'll try my best — and even failure is part of growth."

Step 6: Share or Reflect

If you're working with a partner or group, share your thoughts and reframes. If you're working alone, read them out loud to yourself to reinforce the new narrative.

Why This Exercise Works

- Builds self-awareness — You can't fix what you don't see.

- Strengthens the inner coach — The more you practice reframing, the stronger your positive inner voice becomes.

- Weakens negative programming — When you challenge and reframe negative thoughts, you weaken the neural pathways that reinforce them.

Mindset in Action

This is the work. Cultivating a growth mindset isn't about one-time changes — it's about consistently observing, challenging, and shifting the way you think.

Part 1 gave you the tools — but now you need to apply them. Part 2 will focus on building a sustainable growth mindset — so that confidence, resilience, and success become your default state.

You've already proven you're capable of changing how you think. Now it's time to build on that foundation and unlock your full potential.

Next up: Chapter 5 — Fixed vs. Growth Mindset: Choosing the Path of Expansion

Let's get to work.

PART II

Chapter 5:
Fixed vs. Growth Mindset Choosing the Path of Expansion

Now that you've built a foundation of self-awareness and started to reframe negative thought patterns, you're ready for the next major shift: adopting a growth mindset. This is the moment where you stop just reacting to life — and start intentionally expanding your capacity for success, confidence, and resilience.

If Part 1 was about uncovering the patterns of your mind, Part 2 is about training your mind to work in your favor. And the key to that shift lies in understanding the difference between a fixed mindset and a growth mindset — and consciously choosing the path of expansion.

What is a Fixed vs. Growth Mindset?

Dr. Carol Dweck, a psychologist and researcher, introduced the concept of fixed and growth mindsets through her groundbreaking research on motivation and success.

At the core of her findings is this truth:

- Your beliefs about your ability to grow, learn, and succeed directly influence your outcomes. Let's break down the difference between the two mindsets:
- Growth Mindset
    - Believes that skills, intelligence, and abilities can be developed through effort, learning, and persistence.
    - Sees challenges as opportunities to grow.
    - Views failure as feedback, not as proof of incompetence.
    - Embrace effort as part of the process.

Example: "I didn't get the job, but now I know how to improve for the next opportunity."

- Fixed Mindset
    - Believes that intelligence, talent, and ability are fixed traits — you either have it or you don't.
    - Sees challenges as threats to self-worth.
    - Views failure as proof of inadequacy.
    - Avoids effort because it threatens self-image.

Example: "I didn't get the job because I'm not smart enough — I guess I'm just not good at this."

How Mindset Affects Success

The mindset you operate from shapes how you experience life, especially in the face of challenge or failure.

- Learning and Growth
    - Fixed Mindset → "I'm either naturally good at this or I'm not."
    - Growth Mindset → "I can improve through practice."
- Handling Failure
    - Fixed Mindset → Failure = Proof that you aren't capable.
    - Growth Mindset → Failure = Opportunity to learn and adjust.
- Taking Risks
    - Fixed Mindset → Avoids risks to protect self-image.
    - Growth Mindset → Takes risks because growth comes from discomfort.
- Feedback
    - Fixed Mindset → Takes feedback as a personal attack.
    - Growth Mindset → Takes feedback as useful information for improvement.

Example: Fixed vs. Growth Mindset in Action

Imagine two people, Alex and Jordan, apply for the same job. Both make it to the final round but ultimately don't get hired.

Alex (Fixed Mindset):

- Thought → "I knew I wasn't good enough."
- Emotion → Defeated, ashamed.

- Behavior → Stops applying for jobs, avoids future opportunities.

Jordan (Growth Mindset):

- Thought → "I learned a lot from that experience."
- Emotion → Disappointed but motivated.
- Behavior → Adjusts their approach, applies again with more preparation.

Outcome?

- Alex remains stuck.
- Jordan eventually lands a better job because they adjusted and persisted.

How a Fixed Mindset Develops

A fixed mindset doesn't come from thin air — it's often conditioned through life experiences.

- Early Labeling
    - If you were labeled as "smart," "gifted," or "talented," you might have developed the belief that success is based on natural ability rather than effort.
    - On the flip side, if you were labeled as "slow" or "not creative," you might have internalized the idea that you have permanent limitations.

Example:

- Being told, "You're so smart!" → May lead to fear of failure (because failing would mean you're "not smart").

- Being told, "You're not good at math." → May lead to avoidance of math challenges.
- Perfectionism and Fear of Failure
    - If you were taught that failure is unacceptable, you may have developed the habit of avoiding anything that might lead to failure.
    - Fixed mindsets often show up as perfectionism — because avoiding imperfection feels safer than trying and failing.
- Social and Cultural Pressure
    - Society tends to celebrate "natural talent" over effort.
    - We admire prodigies but overlook the hours of training behind mastery.
    - This reinforces the idea that success = natural ability — rather than consistent work.

Shifting from a Fixed to a Growth Mindset

The good news? A fixed mindset is learned — which means it can be unlearned. You're not locked into your current mindset — you can train yourself to adopt a growth-focused mentality.

1. Redefine Success

Instead of defining success as "perfection" or "winning," define it as:

- Learning something new
- Taking action despite discomfort

- Showing up with intention
- Growing from setbacks

Example:

- Fixed Mindset → Success = Getting hired
- Growth Mindset → Success = Applying with confidence and learning from the interview

2. Normalize Effort

Effort isn't proof that you're not good enough — it's proof that you're growing.

- Talent without effort is wasted potential.
- Consistent effort beats natural talent every time.

Example:

- Fixed Mindset → "If I were good at this, it would be easy."
- Growth Mindset → "I'm improving because I'm putting in the work."

3. Change Your Relationship with Failure

Failure is not a statement about your ability — it's feedback about your strategy.

- Failure = Proof that you're trying.
- Failure = Opportunity to adjust and improve.

Example:

- Fixed Mindset → "I failed, so I'm not capable."

- Growth Mindset → "I failed, so now I know what to adjust."

4. Seek Feedback Instead of Validation

People with a fixed mindset seek validation — they want to be told they're good enough.

People with a growth mindset seek feedback — they want to know how to improve.

Example:

- Fixed Mindset → "Did I do a good job?"
- Growth Mindset → "How can I improve?"

5. Adopt the "Not Yet" Mentality

When you catch yourself saying, "I can't do this," add the word "yet."

- "I'm not good at public speaking." → "I'm not good at public speaking yet."
- "I don't know how to do this." → "I don't know how to do this yet."

Home Exercise: Fixed vs. Growth Mindset Inventory

1. Write down a challenge or goal you've been avoiding.
2. Identify the fixed mindset thought behind that avoidance.
3. Reframe the thought using growth mindset language.
4. Take one small action toward the goal.
5. Write down what you learned — even if it didn't go perfectly.

Example:

- Challenge: Starting a business
- Fixed Mindset Thought: "I'm not cut out for this."
- Growth Reframe: "I can figure this out step by step."
- Action: Research business licenses
- Learning: "I now understand the licensing process — I'm making progress."

Expansion Over Limitation

Shifting from a fixed to a growth mindset doesn't happen overnight — but it starts with the choice to expand.

- Choose effort over ease.
- Choose learning over perfection.
- Choose feedback over validation.
- Choose persistence over immediate success.

In the next chapter, we'll go deeper into how to embrace setbacks and failures — and use them as stepping stones to growth. Because a growth mindset isn't about avoiding failure — it's about learning how to grow through it.

Because growth isn't a destination — it's a process.

Chapter 6: Reframing Failure — Turning Setbacks into Stepping Stones

By now, you've learned that the difference between a fixed mindset and a growth mindset comes down to how you interpret challenges and setbacks. A person with a fixed mindset sees failure as a personal flaw — proof that they aren't good enough. But a person with a growth mindset views failure as a learning experience — a stepping stone toward progress.

The truth is, failure is inevitable. You will face setbacks, rejection, and disappointment in every part of life — relationships, career, personal growth, and beyond. But what determines your success is not **if** you fail — but **how you respond** when you fail.

This chapter is about mastering that response. When you stop seeing failure as an identity statement (*"I'm a failure"*) and start seeing it as feedback (*"That strategy didn't work"*), you unlock a new level of emotional resilience and mental strength.

Reframing failure isn't about pretending that setbacks don't hurt — they do. It's about learning to interpret failure in a way that empowers you rather than defeats you. When you shift how you define and respond to failure, you remove one of the biggest mental blocks standing between you and success.

Why We Fear Failure

Before we can learn how to reframe failure, we need to understand why it feels so threatening. The fear of failure is rooted in both **psychology** and **social conditioning**.

1. Evolutionary Programming

    - Your brain is wired for **survival**, not success.

    - Thousands of years ago, failure often meant physical danger or rejection from the tribe — which could be life-threatening.

    - This is why public speaking or starting a business can trigger a fight-or-flight response — your brain senses it as a threat to your social standing and survival.

2. Social Conditioning

    - Society tends to reward success and punish failure.

    - From school to work to social media, we are conditioned to associate failure with shame and inadequacy.

    - This creates a culture where people avoid taking risks to protect their ego.

Example:

- Getting a bad grade in school → Seen as a sign you're "not smart" rather than an opportunity to learn.

- Losing a game → Seen as personal weakness rather than part of the learning curve.

3. Perfectionism

    - Perfectionism creates an unhealthy relationship with failure because it sets unrealistic standards.
    - When you expect perfection, even small mistakes feel like catastrophic failures.
    - Perfectionism leads to **paralysis** — the fear of making mistakes keeps you from trying at all.

Example:

- Avoiding writing a book because you fear it won't be "perfect."
- Not applying for a job because you don't meet 100% of the qualifications.

Why Failure Is Necessary for Success

What separates successful people from everyone else isn't the absence of failure — it's their ability to **use failure** to grow and improve.

1. Failure Provides Feedback

Failure is a teacher. It provides valuable data about what worked, what didn't, and how you can adjust your approach.

Example:

- Launching a business that doesn't succeed teaches you where the gaps in your strategy were.
- Rejection from a job interview reveals what skills you need to improve.

2. Failure Builds Resilience

Every time you recover from failure, you strengthen your mental and emotional resilience.

- You teach yourself that setbacks are temporary.
- You build confidence in your ability to handle difficult situations.

Example (Career):

- Getting rejected from five jobs but applying again anyway builds emotional toughness and adaptability.
- Each application teaches you something about your interview strategy or your resume — and every rejection brings you closer to the right opportunity.

Example (Entrepreneurship):

- A new business owner launches a product that doesn't sell well.
- Instead of quitting, they adjust the marketing strategy based on customer feedback.
- The revised product resonates with the audience — and sales increase.

3. Failure Breaks the Illusion of Perfection

Once you fail and survive, you realize that failure isn't as catastrophic as you imagined.

- This reduces the emotional charge around failure.
- You stop fearing failure — and you start using it as a tool.

Example:

- After bombing your first public speaking event, you realize that the world didn't end — and you can now improve your delivery.

How to Reframe Failure

The difference between a growth and fixed mindset is not whether you fail — it's how you **interpret** and **respond** to failure.

Here's how to shift from a fear-based response to a growth-based one:

1. Separate Your Identity From the Outcome

You are not your failure.

- Failing at something does not mean you are a failure.
- You need to separate **who you are** from **what happened.**

Example:

- Fixed Mindset → "I'm a failure because I didn't get the job."
- Growth Mindset → "That strategy didn't work, but I am still capable."

2. Treat Failure as Data, Not Judgment

Failure is not a statement about your worth — it's information about what didn't work.

- When you view failure as data, you become curious rather than defensive.
- Curiosity fuels growth; defensiveness fuels shame.

Example:

- "Why didn't this work?" → Insightful
- "Why am I so bad at this?" → Defeating

3. Ask Better Questions

Instead of asking, *"Why did I fail?"* ask:

- *What can I learn from this?*
- *What would I do differently next time?*
- *What part of this experience was in my control?*

Example:
Instead of → "Why am I so bad at relationships?"
Ask → "What patterns am I repeating that aren't serving me?"

4. Normalize Failure

You cannot grow without failing.

- Failure is not an exception — it's part of the process.
- The most successful people in the world failed — a lot.

Example:

- Michael Jordan was cut from his high school basketball team.
- Steve Jobs was fired from his own company before rebuilding Apple.

5. Take Small, Intentional Risks

The more you expose yourself to low-stakes failure, the less power failure holds over you.

- Taking small risks builds emotional resilience.

- Success builds confidence — and failure becomes a learning opportunity.

Example:

- Start by speaking in small groups before doing a keynote.
- Publish a small article before writing a book.
- Test a product with a small audience before scaling it.

Growth-Focused Reframing Examples

Here are some examples of how to shift your response to failure:

Fixed Mindset Thought	Growth Mindset Reframe
"I'm not good at this."	"I'm learning how to get better."
"I failed — I'm not cut out for this."	"I'm figuring out what works and what doesn't."
"Everyone saw me fail."	"I had the courage to try."
"I don't have what it takes."	"I'm developing the skills I need to succeed."
"This didn't work out."	"This showed me what to adjust next time."

Home Exercise: Failure Reflection and Reframing

1. Think of a recent failure or setback.
2. Write down your initial emotional reaction and thoughts about the failure.
3. Identify whether those thoughts are rooted in a fixed or growth mindset.
4. Reframe the failure using growth mindset language.
5. Write down 2–3 adjustments you can make based on what you learned.

Example:

- **Failure:** Didn't get hired for a job.
- **Initial Thought:** "I'm not qualified enough."
- **Reframe:** "I didn't get the job, but I learned how to improve my interview skills."
- **Adjustments:** Practice answering common questions, research the company more deeply next time.

Failure Is a Tool, Not a Threat

Failure is not your enemy — it's your greatest teacher. When you shift your relationship with failure, you unlock new levels of confidence, creativity, and persistence.

The goal isn't to avoid failure — it's to get so comfortable with it that it no longer controls you.

In the next chapter, we'll explore another key growth mindset principle — how to regulate your emotions so that setbacks don't derail your progress.

Because success isn't about avoiding failure — it's about learning how to rise after you fall.

Chapter 7: Emotional Regulation — Mastering Your Reactions

So far, you've learned how to shift your mindset from fixed to growth, and how to reframe failure as feedback rather than defeat. But even with these mindset shifts, there's one major obstacle that can still derail your progress: **your emotional reactions**.

We've all experienced those moments when emotions take over — anger, frustration, sadness, disappointment — and suddenly, logical thinking flies out the window. Even with the best intentions and the strongest mindset, unmanaged emotional reactions can cause you to make impulsive decisions, retreat into old patterns, or even give up entirely.

This is where **emotional regulation** becomes essential.

Emotional regulation is the ability to manage your emotional state in real time — to stay calm, grounded, and intentional, even when things don't go as planned. It's not about suppressing your emotions or pretending you don't feel them — it's about learning how to sit with them, understand them, and respond intentionally rather than react impulsively.

Mastering emotional regulation allows you to handle setbacks without spiraling into self-doubt, stay focused under pressure, and maintain confidence even when things get uncomfortable. In short — it allows you to **stay in control** of your mindset, no matter what life throws at you.

Why Emotional Regulation Matters

Emotions are powerful — but they're not meant to control you. The problem is that most people's emotional responses are **automatic** — they're shaped by past experiences, conditioning, and even evolutionary biology.

When you learn to regulate your emotional state, you gain the ability to:

- Think clearly under pressure.
- Make rational, confident decisions even when stressed.
- Stop reacting impulsively to negative situations.
- Bounce back from setbacks faster.

In other words, emotional regulation is the difference between **acting intentionally** and **reacting emotionally**.

How Emotional Reactions Are Formed

To regulate your emotional reactions, you first need to understand where they come from.

1. The Amygdala and Fight-or-Flight Response

Your brain's emotional response system is controlled by the **amygdala** — a small, almond-shaped part of the brain responsible for detecting threats and triggering survival instincts.

When the amygdala senses a threat (real or perceived), it activates the **fight-or-flight** response:

- Increased heart rate
- Tense muscles
- Racing thoughts
- Heightened emotional sensitivity

This response is designed to protect you from physical danger — but in modern life, your brain can't tell the difference between a real threat (like a predator) and a psychological one (like public speaking).

Example:

- Rejection from a job interview → Amygdala interprets this as a threat → Triggers fight-or-flight → Emotional response = panic, self-doubt, anger.

2. Emotional Memory and Conditioning

Your emotional responses are also shaped by past experiences.

- If you were embarrassed giving a presentation as a child, your brain might now associate public speaking with danger — triggering anxiety every time you step in front of a group.

- If you experienced rejection in relationships, your brain might associate vulnerability with pain — making it hard to open up emotionally.

Example:
- Childhood: Teacher criticizes you in front of the class → Emotional memory = shame and embarrassment.
- Adulthood: Boss gives you constructive feedback → Amygdala recalls past emotional memory → Triggers defensive reaction.

3. Negative Thought Patterns

Once the amygdala activates an emotional response, your mind follows with reinforcing thoughts:

- *"I'm not good enough."*
- *"This always happens to me."*
- *"I'll never succeed."*

This creates a loop where negative thoughts reinforce emotional responses — and emotional responses reinforce negative thoughts.

Example:
Emotional Trigger → Anxiety before a presentation.
Thought → "I'm going to mess this up."
Behavior → Avoidance or poor performance.
Outcome → Reinforces fear of public speaking.

The Goal: Respond, Don't React

The key to emotional regulation is learning how to **create space** between the emotional trigger and your response.

- Reacting = Automatic, emotional response driven by the amygdala.
- Responding = Thoughtful, intentional action shaped by your higher brain (prefrontal cortex).

Example:
Someone criticizes your work.
Reaction = Get defensive and argue.
Response = Take a breath, listen, and decide how to adjust.

The goal is not to eliminate emotional responses — that's impossible. The goal is to become aware of them and choose your response rather than letting your emotions control you.

How to Build Emotional Regulation

Emotional regulation is a skill — which means you can strengthen it through practice. Here's how:

1. Create Space with Deep Breathing

The fastest way to interrupt the fight-or-flight response is through controlled breathing.

- Deep breathing signals to the brain that you are safe — which calms the amygdala and reduces emotional intensity.
- When you control your breath, you regain control of your emotional state.

How to Practice:

- Inhale for 4 counts → Hold for 4 counts → Exhale for 6 counts.
- Repeat for 1–2 minutes or until you feel calmer.

2. Name the Emotion

Research shows that simply naming your emotions reduces their intensity.

- When you name the emotion, you shift control from the emotional brain (amygdala) to the thinking brain (prefrontal cortex).
- Naming the emotion helps you detach from it.

Example:

- "I'm feeling anxious right now."
- "I'm feeling frustrated."

3. Challenge the Thought Behind the Emotion

Once you've calmed your body and identified the emotion, question the thought behind it:

- *Is this thought true?*
- *Is it helpful?*
- *What's another way to look at this?*

Example:

- Thought → "I'm going to fail this test."
- Challenge → "I've studied hard and prepared for this."

4. Focus on What You Can Control

Emotions often spiral when you focus on things you can't control.

- Bring your attention back to what you *can* influence.
- Taking even small action helps regain a sense of control.

Example:

- Can't control → How the interviewer responds.
- Can control → How you prepare and present yourself.

5. Use Visualization to Anchor Confidence
    1. Close your eyes and visualize a successful outcome.
    2. See yourself handling the situation with calm and confidence.
    3. This primes your brain to approach the situation with confidence rather than fear.

Example:

- Before a presentation, visualize yourself speaking clearly, answering questions confidently, and feeling calm.

Examples of Emotional Regulation in Action
Here's how emotional regulation looks in real situations:

Situation	Reaction	Response
Boss gives you negative feedback	Get defensive, shut down	Take a breath, listen fully, ask questions
Business deal falls through	Panic, doubt, self-blame	Reflect on lessons, adjust strategy, try again
Argument with partner	Yell, blame	Pause, take a breath, listen actively, respond calmly
Public speaking	Freeze, forget lines	Take a breath, visualize success, slow down

Home Exercise: The Emotional Reset Practice

1. Think of a recent situation where you reacted emotionally.

2. Write down:
    - The emotional trigger.
    - The reaction you had.
    - The thoughts that followed.

3. Now, rewrite the scenario with an intentional response:
    - How could you have responded differently?
    - What thought could have replaced the emotional reaction?

4. Practice the new response mentally so that next time, you're ready.

Mastering Your Emotions = Mastering Your Mindset

Emotional regulation is about learning to sit with discomfort without losing control. When you master your emotional responses, you gain the power to stay calm under pressure, recover quickly from setbacks, and respond to life with clarity and strength.

In the next chapter, we'll explore how to develop consistent habits that reinforce your growth — so that emotional regulation becomes your default setting rather than just an occasional skill.

Because true power comes not from avoiding emotions — but from learning how to control them.

Chapter 8: Mindful Living — Being Present in a Distracted World

We live in an age of constant noise. Our attention is being pulled in a thousand different directions — phones buzzing with notifications, emails piling up, social media feeds refreshing every few seconds, and the endless stream of news and information. In this chaotic environment, staying present feels almost impossible.

But the ability to be present — to quiet the noise and focus fully on the moment in front of you — is one of the most powerful tools for strengthening your mindset. When you live mindfully, you become more intentional with your thoughts, more aware of your emotions, and more in control of your responses.

Mindful living isn't about slowing down your life or disconnecting from the world — it's about learning how to engage with the world **on your terms**. It's about regaining control over your attention so that you can show up fully and intentionally in every area of your life.

In this chapter, we'll explore what mindfulness really means, why it's essential for a strong mindset, and how you can cultivate mindfulness even in a fast-paced, distraction-filled world.

What Is Mindfulness?

Mindfulness is the practice of bringing your full attention to the present moment — without judgment or distraction.

At its core, mindfulness is about:
Being aware of your thoughts, emotions, and physical sensations.
Accepting what's happening without immediately reacting to it.
Training your mind to focus on the present rather than dwelling on the past or worrying about the future.

It sounds simple — but in a world designed to hijack your attention, it's not easy.

The Science of Mindfulness

Mindfulness isn't just a wellness trend — it's backed by neuroscience. Research shows that mindfulness strengthens the **prefrontal cortex** (the part of the brain responsible for decision-making, emotional regulation, and focus) while reducing activity in the **amygdala** (the part of the brain that triggers stress and fear responses).

Studies have found that mindfulness:

- Reduces stress and anxiety.
- Improves focus and concentration.
- Enhances emotional regulation and resilience.
- Increases overall happiness and life satisfaction.

In other words — mindfulness literally rewires your brain to handle stress more effectively and to stay emotionally balanced even in difficult situations.

Why We Struggle to Stay Present

The modern world is designed to pull us away from mindfulness. We are constantly surrounded by distractions and overstimulation — which creates a state of chronic mental and emotional fragmentation.

1. The Dopamine Loop

Your brain is wired to seek pleasure — and modern technology has exploited that wiring.

- Social media, emails, and notifications trigger dopamine (the brain's reward chemical).
- Every time you check your phone and see a like or a message, you get a small dopamine hit — which reinforces the habit of checking your phone again.
- Over time, this creates a loop where your brain is constantly searching for the next hit of stimulation.

Example:

- You're working on an important project → Phone buzzes → You check it → 20 minutes later, you're scrolling through TikTok wondering where the time went.

2. Multitasking and Mental Overload

Modern life rewards multitasking — but the human brain isn't built for it.

- Every time you switch between tasks, your brain burns extra energy.

- Multitasking increases mental fatigue and reduces overall focus and efficiency.
- Research shows that multitasking reduces productivity by **up to 40%**.

Example:

- You're listening to a podcast while answering emails and scrolling through Instagram.
- None of the tasks get your full attention — and the result is shallow engagement and mental exhaustion.

3. Constant Mental Time Travel

Your mind naturally wanders — either toward the past or the future.

- Thinking about past mistakes → Triggers regret and self-criticism.
- Worrying about the future → Triggers anxiety and fear.
- Rarely do we sit fully in the present without judgment.

Example:

- Instead of enjoying dinner with a friend, you're thinking about tomorrow's meeting or replaying a mistake you made earlier.

The Power of Being Present

When you train yourself to live mindfully, you shift from a state of reaction to a state of presence. This allows you to:

- Respond rather than react to emotional triggers.
- Engage more deeply in conversations and relationships.

- Improve focus and productivity by working with greater clarity.
- Experience more peace and fulfillment in everyday life.

Mindfulness strengthens your mindset because it gives you back control over your attention. When you're present, you are no longer at the mercy of thoughts, emotions, or distractions — you become the driver of your mind rather than the passenger.

How to Cultivate Mindfulness in Daily Life

Mindfulness is a skill — and like any skill, it requires practice. Here's how you can strengthen your ability to stay present, even in a noisy world:

1. Practice Intentional Breathing

Your breath is one of the most powerful tools for grounding yourself in the present moment.

- Deep, intentional breathing activates the parasympathetic nervous system (the body's relaxation system).
- Focusing on your breath helps pull your attention away from mental noise and back to the present.

How to Practice:

1. Close your eyes and inhale deeply for 4 counts.
2. Hold your breath for 4 counts.
3. Exhale slowly for 6 counts.
4. Repeat for 1–2 minutes.

Use this technique whenever you feel anxious, distracted, or emotionally overwhelmed.

2. The 5-4-3-2-1 Grounding Technique

This technique helps you reconnect with the present moment by engaging your senses.

How to Practice:

1. Name **5 things** you can see.
2. Name **4 things** you can feel.
3. Name **3 things** you can hear.
4. Name **2 things** you can smell.
5. Name **1 thing** you can taste.

This method shifts your focus from mental noise to your immediate surroundings — grounding you in the present.

3. Create "Mindful Moments" Throughout the Day

You don't need to meditate for hours to experience mindfulness. Start by embedding small mindful moments into your day:

- Take 60 seconds of deep breathing before starting work.
- Put your phone away while eating and focus on the flavors and textures of your food.
- Before responding to a stressful email, take a deep breath and ask yourself how you want to respond.

4. Set Boundaries with Technology

If you're constantly connected to your phone, you're constantly disconnected from the present.

- Set "no-phone zones" (like the bedroom or dinner table).

- Turn off non-essential notifications.
- Schedule blocks of "focused work" where you put your phone on airplane mode.

Example:

- Instead of scrolling on your phone before bed, read a book for 20 minutes.

5. Engage Fully in Conversations

Mindful living isn't just about focusing on yourself — it's about showing up fully for others.

- Make eye contact when someone is talking.
- Listen without planning your response.
- Put your phone away during conversations.

Example:

- Instead of thinking about your next meeting, focus entirely on the person in front of you.

Examples of Mindful Living in Action

Situation	Unmindful Response	Mindful Response
Eating dinner	Scrolling through phone while eating	Focusing on the taste and texture of each bite
Conversation with friend	Thinking about your response while they talk	Making eye contact and listening fully
Work project	Multitasking with music and phone notifications	Focusing fully on one task at a time

Home Exercise: Mindfulness Check-In

1. Set a timer for **2 minutes**.
2. Sit comfortably and close your eyes.
3. Take slow, deep breaths and notice:
    - What thoughts are present?
    - What physical sensations are you feeling?
    - What emotions are present?
4. When the timer ends, write down what you noticed.

The goal isn't to control your thoughts — it's to observe them without judgment.

Focus Is Power

Mindfulness is about reclaiming control over your mind and attention. In a world designed to pull you in a thousand directions, the ability to stay grounded and present is a superpower.

When you control your attention, you control your mindset. When you control your mindset, you control your results.

In the next chapter, we'll explore how to turn this clarity and presence into consistent, powerful action — through building habits that reinforce your growth.

Because success starts with showing up — fully and intentionally.

Recap of Part 2:
Cultivating a Growth Mindset

Congratulations on completing **Part 2** of *Mindset Matters*! By now, you've made an important shift from understanding your mindset (in Part 1) to actively **training your mind** to work in your favor.

Part 2 was all about cultivating a **growth mindset** — learning to face challenges with confidence, reframe failure as feedback, and regulate your emotional responses in real time. This is the phase where you stopped letting your mind control you and started taking control of your mental and emotional patterns.

Let's take a moment to reflect on what you've learned and how it all fits together.

Key Takeaways from Part 2

1. Fixed vs. Growth Mindset
    - A **fixed mindset** sees abilities as static — you either have it or you don't.

- A **growth mindset** sees abilities as flexible — you can develop them through effort and practice.
- Shifting to a growth mindset opens the door to progress and resilience.

Example:

- Fixed Mindset → "I'm not good at public speaking."
- Growth Mindset → "I can improve my public speaking with practice."

2. Reframing Failure

- Failure is not a reflection of your identity — it's feedback about your strategy.
- Growth happens through trial, error, and adjustment.
- Every setback contains a lesson that makes you stronger.

Example:

- "I failed the test" → "Now I know where to focus my study efforts next time."

3. Emotional Regulation

- Emotions are not the enemy — but they need to be managed.
- Learning to sit with discomfort and control emotional responses allows you to respond rather than react.
- Deep breathing, naming emotions, and focusing on what you can control are key tools for emotional regulation.

Example:

- Trigger → Harsh feedback from a boss.

- Reaction → Breathe, listen fully, process, and respond thoughtfully.

4. Mindful Living

- Mindfulness strengthens focus, clarity, and emotional balance.
- Being present increases your ability to perform under pressure and connect deeply with others.
- Taking control of your attention reduces stress and increases overall life satisfaction.

Example:

- Instead of worrying about tomorrow's meeting, focus on the person you're talking to **right now**.

How These Pieces Fit Together

Each chapter in Part 2 gave you a specific mental tool — but the real power comes from combining them into a single, fluid mindset strategy:

Growth Mindset → Sees challenges as opportunities for improvement.

Reframing Failure → Helps you extract value from setbacks and keep going.

Emotional Regulation → Keeps you grounded and in control during difficult moments.

Mindful Living →Trains your focus so you can stay present and perform at your best.

When you apply these principles together, you create a **mental framework** that allows you to grow through any situation — not just survive it.

Home Exercise: The Mindset Reset Challenge

This exercise will help you integrate all the lessons from Part 2 and train your mind to handle setbacks, emotional triggers, and distractions with confidence and clarity.

Step 1: Identify a Recent Challenge

Think about a recent challenge, failure, or emotional trigger that affected you negatively.

- A rejection?
- A mistake at work?
- A difficult conversation?

Step 2: Reflect Using the Four-Part Mindset Framework

Use the tools from Part 2 to process the situation:

1. **Growth Mindset** – How can you view this situation as an opportunity to grow?
   Example: "I didn't get the job — now I know what to work on for next time."

2. **Reframing Failure** – What specific lesson can you take from this experience?
   Example: "My answers weren't as strong as they could have been — I'll improve my preparation."

3. **Emotional Regulation** – What emotional reaction did you experience? How could you have responded more thoughtfully?
   Example: "I felt frustrated and discouraged — next

time, I'll take a breath and remind myself that one setback doesn't define my ability."

4. **Mindful Living** – How can you stay focused and present moving forward?
   Example: "Instead of obsessing over the rejection, I'll focus fully on preparing for the next opportunity."

Step 3: Plan Your Next Action

Take one small action based on what you learned.

- If you got rejected from a job → Apply for another one.
- If you got critical feedback → Adjust your strategy and try again.
- If you felt overwhelmed → Use a mindfulness technique to regain focus.

Step 4: Track Your Wins

Every time you successfully apply this framework, write it down.

- The more you reinforce positive patterns, the faster they become your default setting.

Group Version of the Exercise

This exercise works well with others too:

- Pair up with a friend or colleague.
- Share a recent challenge.
- Take turns guiding each other through the four-step process.
- Offer each other feedback and support.

Example of the Mindset Reset Framework in Action

Situation:
You give a presentation at work and stumble through part of it.

Growth Mindset: "Public speaking is a skill — and I can improve with practice."
Reframing Failure: "I need to prepare better next time. Now I know which areas to strengthen."
Emotional Regulation: Take a breath, calm down, and remind yourself that it's one event — not a reflection of your worth.
Mindful Living: Instead of replaying the mistake, focus on preparing confidently for the next presentation.

Outcome?

- You've learned from the experience.
- You've managed your emotions.
- You've created a strategy for next time.

Why This Exercise Works

- Combines all four tools into a single strategy.
- Builds resilience through reflection and action.
- Reinforces confidence and emotional control.
- Strengthens long-term emotional intelligence and focus.

You've Built the Mental Foundation — Now It's Time to Expand

Part 2 gave you the mental tools to handle challenges, setbacks, and emotional triggers. But building a strong mindset is not the end goal — it's the foundation for something bigger.

Part 3 is where you'll learn how to **unlock your full potential**. Now that you've mastered your internal world, it's time to focus on external results:

- Building confidence through consistent wins.
- Creating a personal blueprint for success.
- Developing the habits and strategies that lead to long-term growth and fulfillment.

Part 3 is about putting it all together (Unlocking Your Potential) **and stepping fully into the highest version of yourself.**

Because growth isn't just about how you think — it's about how you live.

PART III

Chapter 9: Confidence Through Clarity
Aligning Your Actions with Your Purpose

You've spent the first two parts of this journey building a strong foundation:

- You've mastered your mindset by shifting from fixed thinking to growth thinking.

- You've learned how to regulate your emotions and respond to challenges with intention.

- You've strengthened your focus through mindfulness, creating greater emotional balance.

But now it's time to take it to the next level.

Mindset and emotional control are essential — but they aren't enough on their own. To truly unlock your potential, you need **clarity** — clarity about who you are, what you want, and where you're going. Without clarity, you can work hard but still feel like you're spinning in circles, making progress in the wrong direction.

Confidence comes from clarity — knowing that your daily actions are aligned with your values, your purpose, and your larger vision. When you know exactly what you're working toward — and why it matters — self-doubt fades, motivation increases, and your ability to stay consistent strengthens.

This chapter will help you uncover that clarity — so that you can align your thoughts, emotions, and actions toward a meaningful and purpose-driven life.

Why Confidence Requires Clarity

Confidence isn't just about feeling good about yourself — it's about trusting yourself to make decisions and take action. And that trust comes from having a clear sense of direction.

When you lack clarity, you experience:
❌ Overthinking and hesitation — because you're not sure what to prioritize.
❌ Emotional instability — because you're disconnected from your values and purpose.
❌ Procrastination and inconsistency — because you don't have a clear reason to stay motivated.

But when you have clarity, you experience:
✅ Confidence — because you know what matters and why.
✅ Emotional stability — because you're connected to your deeper sense of purpose.
✅ Consistency — because you have a meaningful reason to keep showing up.

Clarity gives you confidence because it eliminates doubt and hesitation.

Example: Clarity and Confidence in Business

Imagine two entrepreneurs:

Entrepreneur A has no clear business plan. They keep jumping from one strategy to the next based on what they see other people doing. They feel scattered and discouraged because they aren't seeing results.

Entrepreneur B has a clear vision for their business — they know their ideal customer, they've mapped out their strategy, and they've defined success on their own terms. Even when they face setbacks, they stay confident because they trust their plan.

- Confidence doesn't come from getting everything right.
- Confidence comes from knowing exactly what you're working toward and why it matters.

The 3 Levels of Clarity

Clarity doesn't come from a single decision — it's the result of aligning three core areas of your life:

1. Clarity of Identity (Who You Are)

Confidence starts with knowing yourself.

- What are your values?
- What strengths make you unique?
- What motivates you at a deep level?

When you are clear about who you are, you stop comparing yourself to others and start trusting your own instincts.

Example:

- Value: Creativity
- Strength: Public speaking
- Motivation: Helping others grow

If you know that creativity and helping others are core parts of your identity, you'll feel confident building a business around those strengths.

2. Clarity of Vision (Where You're Going)

Confidence requires a clear destination.

- What does success look like for you?
- What are you working toward over the next 1, 5, or 10 years?
- What does your ideal life look like?

When you have a clear vision, you stop getting distracted by comparison or temporary setbacks.

Example:

- Vision: To build a coaching business that empowers 100 people to reach their goals.

When you have a clear goal, you don't get discouraged by slow growth — you focus on the long-term outcome.

3. Clarity of Strategy (How You'll Get There)

Confidence grows when you have a step-by-step plan.

- What daily habits and routines will support your vision?
- What systems will help you stay consistent?
- How will you measure progress?

When you have a clear strategy, you stop overthinking and start executing with confidence.

Example:

- Strategy:

- Write one blog post per week.
- Engage with 20 potential clients every month.
- Track business growth metrics quarterly.

When you know exactly what to do each day, you reduce decision fatigue and build momentum.

How Misalignment Creates Insecurity

When any of these three areas are misaligned, it creates confusion, hesitation, and self-doubt.

🚫 Lack of Identity Clarity → Feeling Lost

- If you don't know who you are, you'll keep chasing other people's definitions of success.

Example:
Trying to build a business because it's trendy — not because it reflects your values or strengths.

🚫 Lack of Vision Clarity → Inconsistent Motivation

- If you don't know where you're going, you'll lose motivation when things get hard.

Example:
Starting a fitness routine without a clear goal → Quitting after two weeks because you aren't seeing results.

🚫 Lack of Strategy Clarity → Overthinking and Hesitation

- If you don't have a plan, you'll waste energy deciding what to do — instead of taking action.

Example:
Spending months "planning" a business but never launching because you aren't sure where to start.

How to Create Confidence Through Clarity

Confidence comes from **alignment** — aligning your identity, vision, and strategy into a single, powerful path forward. Here's how to create that alignment:

1. Define Your Core Values

Start with clarity of identity by defining your values.

- What are the 5 most important values in your life?
- How do these values show up in your daily decisions and actions?

Example:

- Creativity
- Integrity
- Independence
- Growth
- Impact

When you make decisions aligned with your values, you feel grounded and confident.

2. Create a Personal Vision Statement

Write a clear statement that defines where you want to go.

- What does success look like for you?
- How will you know you've achieved it?

Example:
"My vision is to build a business that empowers people to overcome self-doubt and take bold action toward their goals.'

A clear vision gives you direction and motivation.

3. Break It Down Into a Strategy

Confidence grows when you have a clear plan.

- What daily, weekly, and monthly actions will move you toward your vision?
- How will you measure progress?

Example:

- Write one blog post per week.
- Engage with five new potential clients every week.
- Measure business growth monthly.

A clear strategy removes overthinking and increases momentum.

Home Exercise: The Confidence Alignment Blueprint

1. **Define Your Identity**
   - List your top 5 values.
   - Write down your top 3 strengths.
   - Write down what motivates you.
2. **Create Your Vision Statement**
   - What does success look like?
   - How will you feel when you achieve it?
   - Why does it matter to you?
3. **Design a Strategy**
   - What are 3 daily habits that will support this vision?
   - What are 3 weekly goals that will keep you on track?
   - How will you measure success?

Example Blueprint

Values: Creativity, Growth, Impact
Vision: Build a coaching business helping 100 people achieve personal growth.
Strategy:
Post one piece of content weekly.
Schedule five sales calls monthly.
Track income and client satisfaction quarterly.

Confidence Comes From Knowing Your Path.

Clarity creates confidence. When you know who you are, where you're going, and how to get there — you stop overthinking and start executing with focus and strength.

In the next chapter, we'll explore how to take this alignment and build habits that create **consistent, sustainable progress**.

Because confidence isn't about perfection — it's about trusting yourself to handle whatever comes next.

Discipline your thoughts and your destiny will follow.

Chapter 10:
Visualization and Manifestation —
Seeing Your Future Before It Arrives

You've built clarity about who you are, where you're going, and how you'll get there. Now it's time to take that vision and bring it to life.

This is where the power of **visualization and manifestation** comes into play.

Successful people — athletes, entrepreneurs, artists, and leaders — often talk about how they "saw" their success long before it happened. They visualized themselves standing on the podium, signing the business deal, or stepping onto the stage. That's not a coincidence — it's a mental process that primes your brain and body to create the reality you see in your mind.

Manifestation isn't magic — it's science. When you visualize success, you train your mind to align with that reality. You activate the parts of your brain responsible for focus, motivation, and action. Your brain starts looking for opportunities, reinforcing positive behavior, and building the emotional strength needed to sustain progress.

Visualization and manifestation are about **aligning your internal world** (your thoughts, beliefs, and emotions) with your **external goals** — so that you create the reality you desire with clarity and confidence.

In this chapter, we'll explore how visualization works, why it's so powerful, and how to create a manifestation process that actually produces results.

The Science Behind Visualization and Manifestation

Visualization and manifestation aren't just motivational tools — they are backed by neuroscience and psychology.

1. The Reticular Activating System (RAS)

Your brain is constantly bombarded with information — over **11 million bits** of data per second. But you can only consciously process about **50 bits** at a time.

So how does your brain decide what to focus on?
The **Reticular Activating System (RAS)** acts as a filter — directing your attention toward what's most important to you.

When you visualize a specific outcome, your RAS starts looking for evidence and opportunities related to that vision.

- If you focus on success → Your brain will spot opportunities to move toward success.

- If you focus on failure → Your brain will reinforce negative patterns.

Example:

- You visualize yourself landing a new job → You suddenly notice job opportunities and networking events that you previously overlooked.

- You visualize yourself failing → Your mind becomes hypersensitive to criticism and setbacks.

2. Mirror Neurons and Mental Rehearsal

When you visualize yourself performing a task, your brain activates the same neural pathways as if you were actually doing it.

- Visualization strengthens these pathways — making the task feel more natural and automatic when you do it in real life.

- This is why athletes and performers use mental rehearsal before major events — it improves both confidence and execution.

Example:

- A basketball player visualizes sinking free throws → Their brain "practices" the motion even though they aren't physically moving.

- An entrepreneur visualizes delivering a confident pitch → Their brain builds the neural pattern for calm and confidence.

3. Emotional Conditioning

Visualization also activates the emotional centers of the brain — including the **amygdala** (fear and stress) and the **prefrontal cortex** (confidence and decision-making).

- When you imagine success, you create the emotional state that success produces.
- The more you reinforce that emotional state, the more confident and motivated you feel in real life.

Example:
- If you visualize yourself speaking confidently → Your brain experiences the emotion of confidence → You carry that emotional state into the actual presentation.

How Manifestation Works

Manifestation is not about "thinking positive" and waiting for the universe to hand you success — it's about aligning your thoughts, emotions, and actions toward a clear outcome.

Manifestation = Thought + Emotion + Action

1. **Thought** – See the outcome clearly.
2. **Emotion** – Feel the success as if it's already happening.
3. **Action** – Take consistent steps toward the vision.

When you combine these three elements, you shift from wishful thinking to intentional creation.

The Difference Between Visualization and Manifestation

Visualization is about mentally rehearsing the outcome.
Manifestation is about aligning your behavior to create that outcome.

You can visualize yourself running a marathon — but unless you put in the training (manifestation), it won't happen.
You can visualize success in business — but unless you take strategic action, it won't happen.

Visualization primes your mind → Manifestation turns it into reality.

Why Most People Fail at Manifestation

Most people struggle with manifestation because they only focus on one part of the equation:

- **They visualize without action.** → No real-world progress.
- **They take action without belief.** → Leads to burnout and inconsistency.
- **They feel doubt instead of confidence.** → Emotional conflict blocks progress.

True manifestation happens when your thoughts, emotions, and actions are fully aligned.

How to Create a Powerful Visualization and Manifestation Practice

Here's how to build a daily practice that aligns your mind and body with your goals:

1. Create a Clear Mental Picture

The brain needs **specificity** to activate the RAS.

- Instead of visualizing "success," visualize exactly what success looks like.
- Include sensory details — sights, sounds, feelings, and even smells.

Example:

- Instead of visualizing "a successful business," visualize:
    - The office you'll work in.

- The conversations you'll have with clients.
- The feeling of confidence when you see the revenue coming in.

2. Engage Emotion

Feeling is the secret to effective manifestation.

- Imagine the emotional state connected to success — pride, excitement, and confidence.
- When you emotionally connect with the vision, you prime your brain to recreate that feeling in real life.

Example:

- Don't just see yourself winning a race — FEEL the rush of adrenaline as you cross the finish line.

3. Rehearse the Process, Not Just the Outcome

Most people visualize the final result — but the real power comes from visualizing the steps that lead to the result.

- See yourself preparing, adjusting, and overcoming challenges.
- This builds confidence and resilience.

Example:

- Don't just visualize giving a great presentation — visualize practicing, refining, and staying calm under pressure.

4. Repeat Daily

Repetition strengthens neural pathways.

- Spend 5–10 minutes each day visualizing your goal.

- Reinforce the mental image until it feels natural and expected.

Example:

- An entrepreneur visualizes themselves signing a major client → Each time they repeat this, they strengthen their confidence and motivation.

5. Take Aligned Action

Visualization without action = fantasy.

- Take one small action every day toward your vision.
- Consistent effort reinforces the belief that success is inevitable.

Example:

- You visualize running a marathon → You train every morning.
- You visualize a successful business → You reach out to potential clients.

Home Exercise: The Future Self Visualization

1. Sit in a quiet place. Close your eyes.
2. Imagine yourself five years from now:
    - Where are you?
    - What are you doing?
    - Who are you with?
    - How do you feel?
3. Engage all five senses:
    - What does the environment look like?
    - What sounds do you hear?
    - How does it feel emotionally and physically?
4. Now step into that version of yourself:
    - How do they carry themselves?
    - How do they speak?
    - What decisions do they make?
5. Open your eyes and write down the details.
6. Identify ONE action you can take today that aligns with that future version of yourself.

Example:

Future Self Vision:

- Running a successful business
- Traveling internationally for work
- Feeling confident and fulfilled

Action Today:

- Reach out to three potential clients.

What You See, You Become

Visualization is not just about imagining success — it's about training your brain to believe in success. When you see it clearly, feel it deeply, and align your actions with that vision, you make success inevitable.

In the next chapter, we'll explore how to turn that vision into reality by developing consistent habits and systems that drive lasting success.

Because when you can see it in your mind — you can create it in your life.

A healed mindset is a powerful weapon.

Chapter 11: Consistency Over Perfection — Building Lasting Habits

You've learned how to shift your mindset, regulate your emotions, and visualize success. You've gained clarity about your values, vision, and strategy — and you've begun manifesting that vision into reality.

But here's the truth: None of that matters if you can't stay consistent.

Consistency is the bridge between intention and success.

Most people fail not because they lack talent or ambition — but because they lack the ability to stay consistent. They work hard for a week or a month, but when motivation fades or setbacks happen, they quit. They get stuck in the cycle of **starting and stopping**, building momentum and then losing it.

Perfectionism often feeds this pattern — people expect flawless execution, and when they inevitably make a mistake or miss a step, they abandon the process altogether.

But success doesn't come from perfection — it comes from **showing up consistently**, even when it's hard, even when you don't feel like it, and even when progress seems slow.

In this chapter, we'll break down why consistency matters more than perfection, why most people struggle to stay consistent, and how to build habits and systems that create **lasting success**.

Why Consistency Matters More Than Perfection

Perfection is an illusion — but consistency creates real-world results.

1. Consistency Creates Momentum

Progress is built through repetition — not intensity.

- Small, consistent actions accumulate over time.
- Success is the result of tiny, daily choices compounded over weeks, months, and years.

Example:

- Writing for 20 minutes a day = A finished book in six months.
- Exercising for 15 minutes a day = Improved strength and health in a few months.
- Reaching out to one client a day = A growing business within a year.

2. Consistency Builds Identity

Every time you follow through on a habit, you reinforce the belief:

"*I am the type of person who does this.*"

- Writing daily = "*I am a writer.*"

- Working out daily = *"I am healthy and strong."*
- Practicing mindfulness daily = *"I am grounded and calm."*

Your identity shapes your behavior — and consistent action shapes your identity.

Example:

- You're not trying to "become a runner" — you run every day because **you are a runner.**
- You're not trying to "become successful" — you consistently show up and put in the work because **you are a successful person** in the making.

3. Consistency Reduces Mental Fatigue

When you build habits, you reduce the need for willpower and decision-making.

- You don't have to think about it — you just do it.
- This frees up mental energy for creative thinking and problem-solving.

Example:

- Brushing your teeth is automatic — you don't think about it.
- When working out becomes a habit, you don't need motivation — you just show up.

4. Consistency Strengthens Resilience

When you practice consistency, you learn how to push through discomfort and setbacks without quitting.

- Consistent effort teaches you how to handle setbacks without losing momentum.
- It creates emotional toughness — you stop letting temporary failure derail long-term success.

Example:
- If you miss a day at the gym, you don't quit — you just get back on track tomorrow.
- If a product launch fails, you don't shut down the business — you adjust and keep going.

Why Perfectionism Kills Consistency

Most people don't struggle with action — they struggle with expectations.

Perfectionism sets the bar so high that it becomes impossible to succeed consistently.

- If you expect perfect execution → You will quit after the first mistake.
- If you expect immediate results → You will quit when progress is slow.

Perfectionism creates a mindset where:
❌ "If I can't do it perfectly, why bother trying?"
❌ "If I'm not seeing progress, I'm probably doing it wrong."
❌ "If I mess up once, I've ruined everything."

But success is NOT about perfect execution — it's about imperfect repetition.

Example: Perfectionism vs. Consistency

Imagine you want to start running:

Perfectionist Approach:

- Goal → Run 5 miles every day.
- If you miss one day → You feel like a failure and quit.
- Outcome → Inconsistent progress and frustration.

Consistency Approach:

- Goal → Run for 10 minutes every day — no matter how fast or how far.
- If you miss one day → You show up the next day without guilt.
- Outcome → Small wins build into momentum and confidence.

How to Build Consistency Without Falling into Perfectionism

The key to long-term consistency is creating a system that allows you to succeed even when life gets hard, motivation fades, or setbacks happen.

1. Focus on Systems, Not Outcomes

You don't rise to the level of your goals — you fall to the level of your systems.

- Goals define what you want.
- Systems define how you'll get there.

Goal → Write a book.
System → Write for 30 minutes every morning.

Goal → Lose 20 pounds.
System → Exercise for 20 minutes and track meals daily.

Consistency is not about motivation — it's about building systems that make action automatic.

2. Lower the Bar (Start Small)

Perfectionism makes you believe that success requires massive effort — but consistency starts with small, sustainable wins.

- Make the action so small that you can't fail.
- Build confidence through easy wins — then increase intensity gradually.

Example:

- Want to write daily? Start with 5 minutes.
- Want to meditate? Start with 2 minutes.
- Want to exercise? Start with 10 push-ups.

Small wins create momentum — and momentum creates motivation.

3. Follow the "Two-Day Rule"

Consistency does NOT mean perfection.

- It's okay to miss a day — but never miss two in a row.
- Missing two days creates a new pattern — missing one day is just a break.

Example:

- You skip the gym on Monday → Get back on track Tuesday.
- You don't write on Thursday → Write for 5 minutes on Friday.

4. Track Progress Visually

Tracking your progress reinforces the habit and builds motivation.

- Create a habit tracker.
- Check off each day you follow through.
- Seeing a streak builds positive reinforcement and accountability.

Example:

- Calendar with red "X" for each workout.
- Journal where you record daily wins.
- Habit app that tracks your progress.

5. Make Adjustments — But Keep Going

Consistency doesn't mean rigidity.

- If a strategy isn't working, adjust — but don't quit.
- Flexibility allows you to stay consistent even when life shifts.

Example:

- If morning workouts aren't working, try evenings.
- If writing every day feels forced, switch to three times a week.

Home Exercise: The 30-Day Consistency Challenge

1. Choose ONE habit related to your goal.
2. Make it small and manageable.
   - Example: Write for 10 minutes each day.
3. Track it for 30 days.
   - Create a simple chart or use an app.
4. Use the "Two-Day Rule."
   - If you miss a day, reset immediately.
5. After 30 days, reflect:
   - What worked?
   - How can you adjust and improve?

Example:

Habit → Write for 10 minutes every day.
Track → Calendar with daily check marks.
Adjustment → After 30 days, increase to 20 minutes.

Why This Works

Small, manageable actions create long-term progress.
Tracking creates accountability.
The two-day rule prevents "all-or-nothing" thinking.

Consistency Builds Confidence

Confidence isn't built through perfection — it's built through showing up when it's hard, when it's inconvenient, and when progress feels slow.

When you choose consistency over perfection, you build trust in yourself.

- You trust that you will follow through.
- You trust that setbacks won't derail you.
- You trust that small, consistent effort WILL lead to big results.

In the next chapter, we'll explore how to create the external support and accountability that reinforces consistency and fuels long-term growth.

Because success isn't about how hard you work — it's about how consistently you show up.

"

When your mindset aligns with your mission, miracles happen.

Chapter 12: Accountability and Support — The Role of Community in Mindset Growth

You've learned how to shift your mindset, build emotional resilience, and create consistent habits. You've defined your vision, developed clarity, and begun to align your daily actions with your long-term goals.

But there's one more essential element that separates people who thrive from those who struggle to maintain progress: **accountability and support**.

Growth is not a solo journey.

Even the most self-motivated, disciplined people rely on **external support** to stay consistent and keep improving. When you try to grow alone, you face a higher risk of burnout, self-doubt, and inconsistency. But when you surround yourself with the right people — a supportive community and accountability partners — you create an environment where success becomes inevitable.

Success doesn't happen in isolation. It happens through relationships, shared wisdom, and mutual encouragement. The right people will challenge you, keep you focused, and lift you up when you start to doubt yourself.

In this chapter, we'll explore why accountability and support are critical to long-term mindset growth, how to build a powerful support system, and how to leverage accountability to stay consistent even when motivation fades.

Why Accountability and Support Matter

No matter how motivated or independent you are, your environment plays a massive role in shaping your behavior and mindset.

1. Accountability Increases Consistency

When you know that someone else is counting on you or tracking your progress, you are more likely to follow through.

- Accountability creates **external motivation** — even when internal motivation fades.
- The fear of letting someone down increases personal responsibility.

Example:

- You might skip a workout if you're alone — but if you have a workout partner waiting for you, you'll show up.
- You might avoid making sales calls — but if you have to report your weekly numbers to a coach, you'll stay on track.

Accountability reduces procrastination by increasing external pressure.

2. Support Strengthens Resilience

When you face setbacks or failures, having a support system helps you bounce back faster.

- Emotional support reduces the impact of disappointment and frustration.
- Encouragement and advice help you reframe failure and adjust your strategy.

Example:

- After a business deal falls through, a mentor can help you reflect, adjust, and stay motivated.
- After losing a race, a coach can help you process the setback and create a new training plan.

➡️ Support makes setbacks feel temporary rather than permanent.

3. Accountability and Support Create Motivation Through Connection

Humans are wired for connection — we thrive when we feel part of a group.

- Being part of a supportive community increases motivation and emotional strength.
- Seeing other people succeed reinforces the belief that you can succeed too.

Example:

- When you see a fellow entrepreneur hitting their goals, you feel inspired to level up your own performance.
- When you're part of a group training for a marathon, you feel motivated to keep up.

➡ Community creates a shared sense of purpose and momentum.

The Psychology Behind Accountability and Support

Accountability and support work because they leverage two key psychological principles:

1. The Hawthorne Effect

When people know they are being observed, they perform better.

- When you have to check in with someone or report your progress, you naturally increase your effort and focus.
- The act of being watched creates a higher level of responsibility.

Example:

- People are more likely to stick to a workout plan if they're part of a training group.
- Entrepreneurs are more likely to hit their sales goals if they have to report their weekly numbers.

2. Social Proof and Modeling

Seeing other people succeed increases your belief that success is possible.

- When you see others achieving similar goals, it reinforces the belief that you can succeed too.
- Social proof increases confidence and reduces self-doubt.

Example:

- If you see five other people lose weight through a particular program, you're more likely to stick with it.
- If you see fellow entrepreneurs growing their business, you'll feel more confident that you can do the same.

Types of Accountability and Support

Not all accountability is created equal — and different types of support serve different purposes. Here's how to build a balanced system of accountability and support:

1. Peer Accountability

Accountability from people who are at the same level as you creates mutual motivation and shared growth.

- Peer accountability increases motivation because you don't want to fall behind.
- It creates a sense of shared responsibility.

Example:

- Workout partner
- Business mastermind group
- Study group

Peer accountability works because it creates a sense of friendly competition and mutual encouragement.

2. Coaching and Mentorship

Accountability from someone more experienced creates guidance and strategic direction.

- A coach provides expert advice, structure, and high-level feedback.

- A mentor helps you avoid mistakes and stay focused on long-term goals.

Example:

- Hiring a business coach to increase sales.
- Working with a personal trainer to improve athletic performance.
- Seeking advice from a mentor about career decisions.

Coaching increases strategic focus and prevents wasted effort.

3. Community and Group Support

Accountability from a group creates social connection and collective motivation.

- Group support increases emotional resilience and motivation.
- Group accountability reduces feelings of isolation and self-doubt.

Example:

- Group fitness class.
- Entrepreneur mastermind group.
- Online accountability forum.

Community increases motivation and reinforces belonging.

4. Personal Accountability

Accountability to yourself creates intrinsic motivation and self-trust.

- Tracking your progress increases personal responsibility.

- Celebrating wins builds confidence and internal motivation.

Example:

- Habit tracking app.
- Personal journal or goal board.
- Weekly personal check-ins.

Self-accountability increases internal alignment and self-confidence.

How to Build an Effective Accountability System

To maximize accountability and support, you need to create a system that includes **all four types** of accountability. Here's how to design that system:

1. Define the Goal

Clarity is essential — accountability only works if you know exactly what you're working toward.

- What is the specific goal?
- How will you measure success?
- What is the timeline?

Example:

- Goal → Build a six-figure business within 12 months.
- Success → Monthly revenue goal of $8,500.
- Timeline → Quarterly check-ins.

2. Identify Your Accountability Partners

Create a mix of peer, coaching, community, and personal accountability.

- **Peer** → Join a business mastermind.
- **Coach** → Hire a business coach.
- **Community** → Engage in a local or online business group.
- **Personal** → Track progress with a journal.

3. Set a Feedback Loop

Accountability only works if you have a structured system for follow-up.

- Weekly check-ins with a peer.
- Monthly strategy sessions with a coach.
- Daily tracking in a journal or app.

4. Create a Consequence for Inaction

Positive reinforcement and mild consequences increase follow-through.

- Consequence → If you miss a weekly goal, donate to a cause you dislike.
- Reward → If you hit a goal, treat yourself to something meaningful.

5. Adjust and Refine

Not all systems work perfectly — adjust based on what works.

- If peer accountability isn't working, try a coach.
- If the system feels too rigid, make it more flexible.

Home Exercise: Build Your Accountability System

1. Define your goal.
2. Identify 1-2 peers to serve as accountability partners.
3. Seek out a coach or mentor for strategic guidance.
4. Join a group that aligns with your goal.
5. Create a personal tracking system.

Example:

Goal → Land 5 new clients within 90 days.
Peer → Business partner.
Coach → Sales coach.
Community → Entrepreneur group.
Tracking → Weekly goal board.

Success Requires a Team

Growth happens faster — and more consistently — when you have support.

- Your mindset shapes your behavior.
- Consistency creates progress.
- Accountability ensures that you stay on track — even when motivation fades.

In the next chapter, we'll explore how to sustain momentum by aligning your lifestyle with your mindset — so that growth becomes automatic and effortless.

Because success isn't just about effort — it's about building a support system that makes success inevitable.

You don't need a new life —
you need a new lens.

Recap of Part 3: Unlocking Your Potential

Congratulations! You've made it through **Part 3** of *Mindset Matters* — and this is where you've truly stepped into your power. In Part 1, you built the foundation of your mindset. In Part 2, you cultivated the tools to regulate your emotions and create consistency. But **Part 3** was about taking action — aligning your mindset with your goals and beginning to shape your future with intention and confidence.

You've shifted from **internal growth** to **external success**. You've learned how to align your identity, vision, and actions. You've strengthened your belief in yourself — not just by thinking differently, but by showing up differently.

Part 3 was about stepping into the driver's seat of your life.

Let's take a moment to reflect on the key takeaways from Part 3 and how they all connect:

Key Takeaways from Part 3

1. Confidence Through Clarity

- Confidence comes from knowing **who you are**, **what you want**, and **how to get there**.
- When your identity, vision, and strategy align, you eliminate confusion and hesitation.
- Clarity reduces overthinking and increases action.

Example:

- Identity → "I am a writer."
- Vision → "I want to publish a book within 12 months."
- Strategy → "Write for 30 minutes every morning."

When you have clarity, you stop hesitating — you know exactly what you need to do.

2. Visualization and Manifestation

- Visualization primes your brain to recognize opportunities and execute with confidence.
- Manifestation works when thoughts, emotions, and actions align.
- When you see success in your mind first, you strengthen your belief that it's possible.

Example:

- Visualization → Seeing yourself confidently giving a TED Talk.
- Manifestation → Practicing your speech and adjusting based on feedback.

Seeing success before it happens builds confidence and focus.

3. Consistency Over Perfection

- Success comes from small, consistent action — not perfect execution.
- The goal isn't to never fail — it's to keep showing up even when you fail.
- Progress compounds through daily effort.

Example:

- Writing for 10 minutes every day = A finished book in six months.
- Working out 3 times a week = Improved health over time.

Consistency creates progress, even when motivation fades.

4. Accountability and Support

- You are more likely to succeed when you have external accountability.
- A strong support system increases emotional resilience and motivation.
- Success accelerates when you surround yourself with the right people.

Example:

- Peer Accountability → Workout partner.
- Coaching Accountability → Business mentor.
- Group Accountability → Mastermind group.

Growth happens faster when you have others invested in your success.

How It All Connects

The tools from Part 3 form a powerful success cycle:

1. **Clarity** → Knowing exactly what you want and how to get there.
2. **Visualization** → Strengthening belief and emotional alignment.
3. **Consistency** → Taking daily action to reinforce confidence.
4. **Accountability** → Leveraging external support to stay on track.

This cycle allows you to stay focused, motivated, and resilient — even when challenges arise. You've built the mental and emotional framework to keep moving forward no matter what.

Home Exercise: The 30-Day Success Blueprint

This exercise will help you apply the lessons from Part 3 and create a plan for consistent progress over the next 30 days.

Step 1: Define Your Goal

- What is one specific goal you want to accomplish in the next 30 days?
- Make it clear and measurable.

Example:

- Goal → Sign three new clients for your business.
- Goal → Lose 5 pounds.
- Goal → Finish two chapters of your book.

Step 2: Create a Strategy

- Break down the goal into weekly and daily steps.
- Focus on consistent effort — not massive action.

Example:

- Weekly → Reach out to 15 potential clients.
- Daily → Write for 30 minutes.
- Weekly → Work out three times a week.

Step 3: Use Visualization

- Spend 5 minutes each morning visualizing the outcome.
- Feel the success as if it's already happening.

Step 4: Build Accountability

- Find an accountability partner or coach.

- Join a group or mastermind.
- Track your progress daily.

Step 5: Follow the Two-Day Rule

- If you miss a day, that's okay — just don't miss two in a row.

Step 6: Celebrate Wins

- Every week, reflect on what's working.
- Adjust your strategy based on feedback.
- Reward yourself for consistent effort — not just outcomes.

Example Blueprint

Goal → Finish 2 chapters of a book in 30 days.
Strategy → Write for 30 minutes every morning.
Visualization → Imagine yourself holding the finished book.
Accountability → Weekly check-in with a writing coach.
Two-Day Rule → If you miss a day, get back on track immediately.

Group Version of the Exercise

- Pair up with a partner.
- Share your goal and strategy.
- Check in with each other once a week.
- Celebrate progress together.

Why This Works

Clarity reduces overthinking.
Visualization increases confidence.

Consistency builds momentum.
Accountability prevents quitting.

You've Built the Foundation — Now It's Time to Live It

Part 3 was about stepping into action — learning how to create success through consistent effort, emotional strength, and strategic alignment.

Now, it's time for the final step: **embodying the results.**

Part 4 is about learning how to sustain your success and live in alignment with your highest self. You've built the mindset, the habits, and the strategy — now it's time to make this your permanent way of being.

You're no longer building the foundation — now you're living the results.

"

Growth becomes impact when your transformation teaches others how to rise.

PART IV

When mindset becomes lifestyle, change stops being something you chase — and starts being who you are.

Chapter 13: From Mindset to Lifestyle — Embodying Your New Reality

You've done the inner work.
You've shifted from a fixed to a growth mindset.
You've learned how to regulate your emotions, build confidence, and create consistency.
You've started to see tangible results — the business is growing, your relationships are improving, your health is stronger, and your sense of self is clearer than ever.

But here's the truth: **Mindset alone isn't enough.**

Mindset is the starting point — but to create lasting success, you need to translate that mindset into a lifestyle.

A strong mindset helps you make better decisions, stay consistent through challenges, and push through fear and self-doubt. But unless you integrate those mental shifts into your daily life, you risk sliding back into old patterns.

This chapter is about making your mindset permanent. It's about turning confidence and clarity into a lifestyle — a way of being that reflects your highest self in every area of life.

Success isn't just about hitting a goal — it's about **becoming the kind of person** who naturally attracts success.

It's time to stop working on your mindset — and start **living it**.

Why Mindset Shifts Fade

Most personal growth journeys follow a similar pattern:

1. **Initial Excitement** – You feel inspired and motivated to change.
2. **Early Wins** – You see some progress, and your confidence grows.
3. **Resistance and Setbacks** – Life gets busy, motivation fades, and you start missing steps.
4. **Regression** – Without reinforcement, you slip back into old habits and patterns.

This happens because:

- Your **environment** hasn't changed.
- Your **habits** haven't become automatic.
- Your **identity** hasn't fully aligned with your new mindset.

Mindset without lifestyle integration = temporary progress.

Example: Business and Fitness

- You shift your mindset to believe you can build a successful business → You land a few clients.

- But when you stop taking consistent action or lose motivation, you start doubting yourself again → You fall back into overthinking and hesitation.

- You shift your mindset to believe you're capable of improving your health → You lose 10 pounds.

- But when stress hits and your old eating habits creep back, you regain the weight.

If you don't anchor your new mindset into a consistent lifestyle, you stay stuck in the cycle of **progress and regression**.

Mindset → Identity → Lifestyle

The key to sustaining growth is moving from mindset change to **identity shift** — and then reinforcing that identity through consistent action.

Mindset → The shift in thinking. *"I am capable of running a successful business."*

Identity → The belief about yourself. *"I am an entrepreneur."*

Lifestyle → Daily habits that reflect that identity. *"I take consistent action to grow my business every day."*

When you align your lifestyle with your identity, success becomes automatic — because you no longer have to "work" to stay consistent. You simply act in alignment with the person you've become.

Why Identity Change Matters

Your mind is designed to seek alignment between your **beliefs** and your **actions**.

When your identity and behavior are aligned, you feel confident and powerful.
When your identity and behavior are misaligned, you feel doubt and confusion.

Example:

- If you believe you're a "fit person," going to the gym feels natural.
- If you believe you're "bad with money," managing finances feels uncomfortable.

When you shift your **identity**, your actions follow automatically.

Old Pattern → Identity Conflict

Mindset: *"I want to be confident."*
Identity: *"I've always struggled with self-esteem."*
Action: Inconsistent follow-through → Doubt → Lack of results.

New Pattern → Identity Alignment

Mindset: *"I am confident."*
Identity: *"I trust myself to handle any challenge."*
Action: Consistent action → Confidence reinforces itself → Results.

How to Shift From Mindset to Lifestyle

The shift from mindset to lifestyle happens when you integrate your new beliefs and identity into your daily routine and environment.

Here's how to make that shift permanent:

1. Define Your New Identity

Stop thinking about "what you want to accomplish" and start thinking about **who you want to become**.

What kind of person creates the success you desire?
What habits and behaviors does that person embody?
How do they show up in the world?

Example:

- Instead of: *"I want to lose weight."*

- Shift to: *"I am a healthy person."*

- Instead of: *"I want to grow a business."*

- Shift to: *"I am a successful entrepreneur."*

2. Act As If

Once you've defined the identity, begin acting as if you already are that person.

- Make decisions based on that identity.
- Speak, dress, and carry yourself as that person.
- Ask yourself: *"What would a confident/healthy/successful person do?"*

Example:

- Identity → *"I am a writer."*

- Action → Write for 30 minutes every day.

- Identity → *"I am a confident person."*

- Action → Make eye contact and speak with authority.

3. Adjust Your Environment

Your environment shapes your behavior.

- Surround yourself with people who reflect your new identity.
- Remove triggers and distractions that reinforce old patterns.

Example:

- If you want to build wealth → Surround yourself with successful, financially disciplined people.
- If you want to improve your health → Fill your kitchen with healthy food.

4. Build Habits That Reinforce Your Identity

Habits strengthen identity because they create evidence that you are becoming the person you envision.

- Start small and build momentum through daily repetition.
- Focus on effort, not outcomes.

Example:

- Identity → "I am a fit person."
- Habit → 20 minutes of exercise every morning.

- Identity → "I am a successful business owner."

- Habit → Reach out to three potential clients every day.

5. Celebrate Wins and Reinforce Identity

Every small success reinforces your new identity.

- Track progress and reflect on wins.
- Celebrate effort as much as outcomes.

Example:

- Identity → "I am a leader."
- Celebration → Acknowledge when you make a difficult but necessary decision.

Home Exercise: Lifestyle Integration Plan

This exercise will help you shift from mindset to lifestyle by aligning your daily habits with your new identity.

Step 1: Define Your New Identity

- Who do you want to become?
- Write a clear identity statement.

Example:
"I am a confident and successful business owner."

Step 2: Identify 3 Core Habits

- What daily actions will reinforce that identity?

Example:
Write for 20 minutes.
Reach out to three potential clients.
Exercise every morning.

Step 3: Design Your Environment

- Remove distractions or triggers that don't reflect your identity.
- Add elements that support your success.

Example:

- Remove junk food from your kitchen.
- Create a dedicated writing space.

Step 4: Celebrate Small Wins

- Create a weekly check-in to reflect on progress.
- Acknowledge effort, not just outcomes.

Step 5: Commit to 30 Days

- Follow through daily for 30 days.
- If you miss a day, apply the Two-Day Rule (don't miss two in a row).

Example Lifestyle Integration Plan

Identity → "I am a successful entrepreneur."
Habits → Daily outreach, content creation, personal development.
Environment → Create an organized home office.
Reward → Weekly reflection and celebration.

Becoming the Person Who Wins

True transformation happens when mindset becomes identity — and identity becomes action.

- You are no longer "trying" to succeed — you are succeeding because it's who you are.
- Confidence isn't about what you know — it's about how you live.

In the next chapter, we'll explore how to sustain this empowered lifestyle over the long term — even when life tests you.

Because success isn't just what you do — it's who you are.

What you speak to your mind,
your life learns to repeat.

Chapter 14: Navigating Challenges — When Life Tests Your Mindset

You've done the work.
You've shifted your mindset, created clarity, and built confidence.
You've established consistent habits and aligned your lifestyle with your identity.

But now life is about to throw you a test.

Because no matter how much inner work you've done, no matter how clear your vision is, and no matter how consistent you've been — life will challenge you.

Setbacks, failures, and unexpected obstacles are inevitable.

- A business deal falls through.
- A health setback slows your progress.
- A personal relationship breaks down.
- Financial pressure increases.

Challenges are not a matter of *if* — they're a matter of *when*.

The difference between people who succeed and people who stay stuck is NOT that successful people avoid challenges — it's that they know how to handle them when they show up.

This chapter is about preparing yourself for those inevitable tests — so that when life challenges you, you don't crumble or fall back into old patterns. Instead, you'll learn how to face those challenges with strength, resilience, and emotional control — and keep moving forward.

Because true empowerment isn't about avoiding problems — it's about knowing you can handle them.

Why Challenges Trigger Regression

Challenges are so dangerous because they threaten to unravel all the progress you've made.

1. Stress Re-Activates Old Patterns

When you face stress, your brain shifts into survival mode — triggering the amygdala (the fight-or-flight center).

- Your body produces cortisol and adrenaline.
- Logical thinking decreases, and emotional reactivity increases.
- The brain defaults to old coping mechanisms — even if they are unhealthy or ineffective.

Example:

- You've been consistent with your diet → Stress hits → You reach for junk food because that's how you used to cope.

- You've been building confidence in your business → A deal falls through → You spiral into self-doubt and procrastination.

Stress pushes you toward familiar, comfortable patterns — even if they no longer serve you.

2. Fear and Doubt Resurface

Challenges awaken old limiting beliefs:

- *"What if I'm not good enough?"*
- *"What if this means I'm not meant to succeed?"*
- *"What if this is proof that I'm a failure?"*

Your brain interprets setbacks as evidence that your success was a fluke — and tries to pull you back into "safety" by convincing you to quit.

Example:

- A failed business pitch = "Maybe I'm not cut out for this."
- A difficult conversation with a partner = "Maybe I'm not meant to have a healthy relationship."

Doubt and fear make quitting feel safer than continuing.

3. Emotional Overload Undermines Logic

When you face a challenge, your emotional response often overwhelms logical thinking.

- Anger, sadness, or anxiety cloud your decision-making.
- You overreact or underreact.
- You become defensive, withdrawn, or impulsive.

Example:

- A client rejects your offer = You get defensive and close off future conversations.
- A relationship conflict escalates = You shut down emotionally and withdraw.

Emotional overload disconnects you from strategic thinking and self-awareness.

The Key to Overcoming Challenges: Emotional Agility

Emotional agility is the ability to handle emotional discomfort without losing control.

- It's not about suppressing emotions — it's about processing them without letting them dictate your behavior.
- When you develop emotional agility, you create space between stimulus and response — which allows you to respond intentionally rather than react emotionally.

Emotional agility = Mastering your emotional state under pressure.

How to Navigate Challenges Without Losing Momentum

Here's how to strengthen your emotional agility and face challenges without letting them derail you:

1. Pause and Create Space

The moment you feel yourself emotionally triggered: STOP.

- Take a breath.
- Create physical and mental space between the event and your response.

- Emotional reactions are automatic — but intentional responses require a pause.

How to Practice:

- Step away from the situation for 5 minutes.
- Take 3 deep breaths.
- **Name the emotion you're feeling (*"I'm feeling frustrated."*).**

Creating space stops the automatic emotional response and puts you back in control.

2. Identify the Story You're Telling Yourself

Every emotional reaction is fueled by an internal story:

- *"This means I'm not good enough."*
- *"I knew this would happen."*
- *"I always mess things up."*

Your emotional response is not about the event — it's about the meaning you've attached to the event.

How to Practice:

- Ask yourself: *"What's the story I'm telling myself right now?"*
- Challenge the story: *"Is this true?"*
- Replace it with a growth mindset story:
  "This setback doesn't define me — I can adjust and improve."

Example:
Challenge → A failed job interview.
Story → *"I'm not good enough."*

Reframe → *"This is feedback — I know how to improve next time."*

3. Focus on What's in Your Control

Most challenges trigger anxiety because they highlight things you can't control.

- You can't control other people's opinions.
- You can't control every outcome.
- You can't control timing.

What you can control:
Your effort.
Your preparation.
Your response.

How to Practice:

- Make two lists:
    - "What I Can Control"
    - "What I Can't Control"
- Let go of the second list.
- Focus your energy exclusively on the first list.

Example:

- You can't control whether a client says yes — but you can control how prepared you are.

4. Adjust, Don't Abandon

When a challenge disrupts your progress, your instinct might be to give up or shut down.

- Instead of abandoning the goal — adjust the strategy.

- Setbacks often signal that you need to refine your approach.

How to Practice:

- After a setback, ask:
  "What's one thing I can adjust?"
  "What's one lesson I can take from this?"

Example:

- A failed sales pitch → Adjust the script.
- A missed workout → Shorten the routine.
- A difficult conversation → Try a different approach next time.

5. Lean on Your Support System

Challenges feel heavier when you try to carry them alone.

- Reach out to your accountability partner or coach.
- Ask for feedback and perspective.
- Emotional support helps you process setbacks more quickly and return to action.

Example:

- After a business setback → Talk to a mentor about next steps.
- After a personal conflict → Process with a trusted friend.

Support accelerates emotional recovery and keeps you moving forward.

Home Exercise: The Challenge Response Plan

This exercise will help you prepare for and respond to challenges effectively:

Step 1: Identify a Potential Challenge

- What's one area where you expect to face resistance?
- Example: Public speaking, business growth, relationship conflict.

Step 2: Pre-Define Your Response

- How will you respond to this challenge?
- Example: *"If I feel nervous before a presentation, I will breathe deeply and visualize success."*

Step 3: Build a Support Strategy

- Who will you reach out to for support?
- Example: *"If I experience a business setback, I will call my mentor for advice."*

Step 4: Track and Adjust

- After the challenge, reflect:
    - What worked?
    - What needs to adjust?

Challenges Don't Define You — How You Respond Does

Empowerment isn't about avoiding challenges — it's about knowing that you are strong enough to handle them.

- Setbacks are not signs of failure — they are tests of emotional resilience.

- You can't control every challenge — but you can control your response.

In the next chapter, we'll explore how to sustain motivation and momentum — even when challenges keep coming.

Because strength isn't about never falling — it's about rising every time you do.

Healing your mindset plants seeds of possibility in everyone watching you bloom.

Chapter 15: Leaving a Legacy — Impacting Others Through Your Growth

You've come a long way.

You've reshaped your mindset.
You've learned how to handle setbacks with strength and grace.
You've built consistency and confidence through daily action.
You've aligned your habits and lifestyle with your higher self.

But true success isn't just about personal growth — it's about **how you use that growth to impact others**.

Real fulfillment comes not from what you achieve — but from what you give.

- Success satisfies you.
- Contribution fulfills you.

Leaving a legacy is about shifting from personal success to **collective impact**. It's about using your journey — the wins, the failures, the lessons — to inspire, support, and elevate others.

True legacy isn't defined by money or status — it's defined by how you make others feel and how you change the lives around you.

The most powerful thing you can give to the world isn't what you have — it's **who you've become**.

In this chapter, you'll learn how to expand your growth beyond yourself — to lead, mentor, and inspire others. You'll discover how to create a legacy of strength, courage, and transformation that outlives you.

Because the ultimate purpose of personal growth is to create a ripple effect — one that touches lives long after you're gone.

What It Means to Leave a Legacy

A legacy is not about what you accomplish — it's about what you pass on.

- How will people remember you?
- How will your impact continue beyond your lifetime?
- What will people say about how you made them feel?

Success is Temporary — Impact is Permanent

- Money, status, and material success fade.
- But the way you empower others, the lessons you teach, and the love you give live on.

Legacy Is Influence That Outlives You

Your legacy isn't built when you reach the top — it's built through the way you support others while you climb.

- The advice you give.
- The strength you model.

- The opportunities you create for others.

Example:

- A business leader who mentors young entrepreneurs leaves a legacy of confidence and strategy.
- A teacher who empowers students to believe in themselves creates a legacy of self-worth and possibility.

Legacy isn't about what you take with you — it's about what you leave behind.

Why Legacy Matters

Leaving a legacy isn't just about helping others — it strengthens your own mindset and success.

1. Contribution Creates Meaning

Psychologists have found that **contribution** is one of the highest drivers of long-term happiness and fulfillment.

- Achieving personal success feels good — but it's temporary.
- Contribution creates a sense of purpose and lasting fulfillment.

Example:

- Making $100,000 from a business = Satisfying.
- Helping others build businesses that change their lives = Fulfilling.

Contribution shifts your focus from "What can I get?" to "What can I give?"

2. Contribution Strengthens Confidence

Teaching reinforces learning.

- When you share your lessons with others, you deepen your understanding of them.
- Leading others reinforces the belief that you are capable and powerful.

Example:

- Coaching someone through a mindset block strengthens your own emotional resilience.
- Teaching business strategy reinforces your own knowledge of the process.

Empowering others increases confidence in your own expertise.

3. Contribution Builds Emotional Resilience

Helping others creates emotional stability — even during personal challenges.

- When you focus on serving others, you shift out of self-focus and into purpose.
- Contribution reduces anxiety, depression, and overthinking.

Example:

- During a personal setback → Coaching someone through a difficult situation helps you reframe your own challenge.
- Business struggles → Helping someone else strategize reminds you that you are still capable and valuable.

Giving back strengthens emotional stability.

Types of Legacy

Legacy can take many forms — and you have the power to create it in your own unique way.

1. Legacy of Knowledge

    - Sharing your expertise and wisdom.
    - Teaching others how to navigate challenges.
    - Passing down the lessons you've learned.

Example:

- Writing a book.
- Hosting a workshop.
- Mentoring someone through career growth.

2. Legacy of Strength

    - Modeling emotional resilience and mental strength.
    - Teaching others how to handle setbacks and challenges.
    - Showing others that they can rise after they fall.

Example:

- A parent modeling resilience after losing a job.
- A leader maintaining composure during a crisis.

3. Legacy of Opportunity

    - Creating opportunities for others to succeed.
    - Removing barriers and providing access to resources.
    - Helping others step into their potential.

Example:

- A business leader offering internships to underserved communities.
- A teacher helping a struggling student find a scholarship.

4. Legacy of Inspiration

- Motivating others to believe in themselves.
- Empowering others through your story.
- Inspiring others to dream bigger and pursue their goals.

Example:

- A motivational speaker sharing their journey of overcoming adversity.
- A coach helping someone see their value and potential.

How to Build a Legacy That Lasts

Creating a legacy isn't about a single act — it's about showing up consistently and building a life that reflects your highest values.

1. Lead by Example

Your actions will influence people more than your words.

- Show others what strength looks like by living it.
- Be the person you wish you had as a mentor.
- Consistency builds credibility.

Example:

- Don't just teach confidence — embody it.

- Don't just talk about health — live it.

People follow who you are — not just what you say.

2. Share What You've Learned

You've faced challenges, failures, and wins — now pass that wisdom on.

- Be transparent about your struggles.
- Teach others how to avoid the mistakes you made.
- Give others the tools to succeed faster.

Example:

- Write a book.
- Start a podcast.
- Mentor someone 1:1.

Your story will become someone else's survival guide.

3. Create Opportunities for Others

Success feels even better when you create success for others.

- Open doors for others.
- Recommend people for jobs and opportunities.
- Provide mentorship and support.

Example:

- Introduce a young entrepreneur to a key investor.
- Help a colleague build the confidence to apply for a promotion.

Legacy is about building ladders for others to climb.

4. Build Something Bigger Than Yourself

Create something that will outlive you.

- A business that continues to serve others.
- A foundation that funds future growth.
- A piece of art or writing that inspires others for generations.

Example:

- Building a coaching business that continues after you retire.
- Creating a foundation for mental health awareness.

When you create systems that live beyond you, your legacy becomes permanent.

Home Exercise: Legacy Blueprint

This exercise will help you define the legacy you want to create — and start building it today.

Step 1: Define Your Legacy Statement

- How do you want to be remembered?
- What impact do you want to leave behind?
- What values do you want others to carry forward?

Example:
"I want to be remembered as someone who empowered others to believe in themselves and take bold action toward their dreams."

Step 2: Identify Your Legacy Path

- Knowledge → Teach others what you've learned.
- Strength → Model resilience through challenges.
- Opportunity → Create doors for others to walk through.
- Inspiration → Share your story openly.

Step 3: Take One Action Today

- Mentor someone.
- Create content that teaches.
- Recommend someone for an opportunity.
- Share your story vulnerably.

Your Life is Bigger Than You

True empowerment isn't about personal success — it's about lifting others as you rise.

- Success fades — impact lasts.
- Confidence strengthens you — legacy strengthens others.
- Your greatest achievement won't be what you accomplish — it will be how you **empower others** to succeed.

In the next chapter, we'll explore how to maintain momentum and stay grounded as you continue to grow and give back.

Because true success isn't about what you build — it's about what you leave behind.

Chapter 16:
The Lifelong Journey of Mindset Mastery

You've reached the final chapter of *Mindset Matters*.

But the truth is — this isn't the end. It's the beginning.

Mindset mastery isn't a destination — it's a lifelong journey.

- You've built the foundation of a growth mindset.
- You've learned how to regulate your emotions, build confidence, and create consistency.
- You've aligned your life with your identity and vision.
- You've navigated setbacks and learned how to rise after failure.
- And you've begun to create a legacy that will outlive you.

But life will continue to evolve.

- New challenges will arise.
- Your goals and vision will grow and shift.
- New seasons of life will demand new versions of you.

Mastering your mindset means learning how to adapt, evolve and stay grounded through **every phase** of life — not just during moments of success, but also during times of uncertainty and change.

Success isn't about arriving — it's about continuing to rise, no matter what life throws at you.

This chapter is about preparing you for that lifelong journey — so that you don't just succeed once — you keep growing, keep evolving, and keep winning.

Because mindset mastery isn't just about creating success — it's about learning how to sustain it for a lifetime.

What Mindset Mastery Really Means

Mindset mastery isn't about controlling every outcome — it's about controlling your response to every outcome.

It's Not About Avoiding Failure — It's About Learning How to Rise

- Challenges will come — you've learned how to face them with confidence.
- Failure will happen — you've learned how to extract the lesson and keep going.

It's Not About External Success — It's About Internal Strength

- Money, status, and recognition can disappear — but self-trust and emotional resilience remain.

- Confidence isn't about what you've achieved — it's about knowing you can handle whatever comes next.

It's Not About Motivation — It's About Identity

- Motivation fades — but identity drives action.
- When success becomes part of who you are, you no longer need motivation to take action — you simply act in alignment with your identity.

The 5 Core Principles of Lifelong Mindset Mastery

These five principles will serve as your foundation for lifelong growth and success — no matter what season of life you're in.

1. Clarity Creates Confidence

Success requires knowing exactly what you want and why it matters.

- Clarity reduces hesitation and overthinking.
- A clear vision creates a roadmap for daily action.

Example:

- Business growth → Define revenue targets, clients, and services.
- Fitness → Define your health goals and training plan.
- Relationships → Define what kind of partner you want to be.

The clearer the target, the more confidently you'll aim.

2. Consistency Over Perfection

You won't always feel motivated — but consistency keeps you moving forward.

- Small, consistent effort compounds over time.
- Success comes from repetition, not flawless execution.

Example:

- Writing for 15 minutes a day = A finished book in 6 months.
- Making 5 sales calls a week = Business growth over time.
- Showing up for your partner daily = Stronger relationships over time.

Consistency builds momentum — even when motivation fades.

3. Emotional Regulation Over Emotional Reaction

You can't control your emotions — but you can control your response to them.

- Create space between emotion and action.
- Respond with intention rather than reacting impulsively.

Example:

- Frustration at work → Take a breath and process before responding.
- Feeling overwhelmed → Step back, reset, and approach with strategy.

Emotional strength allows you to stay grounded under pressure.

4. Focus on Growth, Not Perfection

Success isn't about never failing — it's about learning from each failure.

- See setbacks as data — not proof of inadequacy.

- Adjust, improve, and keep moving.

Example:
- A failed business pitch = Adjust your strategy and try again.
- A workout plateau = Adjust your routine and keep training.

Growth happens when you stop avoiding failure and start learning from it.

5. Give Back and Create Impact

True success isn't about what you accomplish — it's about how you help others grow.

- Use your knowledge and strength to empower others.
- Create a legacy of confidence, strength, and resilience.

Example:
- Mentoring a younger entrepreneur.
- Helping a friend overcome a mindset block.
- Creating opportunities for others to succeed.

Legacy happens when you lift others as you rise.

The Mindset Mastery Cycle

Mindset mastery is not linear — it's cyclical.

1. **Clarity** → You define your vision and strategy.
2. **Action** → You build consistency through daily effort.
3. **Challenge** → Life tests you with setbacks and failures.
4. **Adjustment** → You refine your strategy and approach.

5. **Growth** → You evolve and expand your capacity.

Then the cycle begins again — each time at a higher level of awareness and strength.

Mastery isn't about avoiding the cycle — it's about learning how to move through it with strength and confidence.

How to Stay Grounded in Lifelong Growth

Mastering your mindset for life requires a few key strategies:

1. Keep Revisiting Your Vision

As you grow, your goals and values will evolve.

- Regularly reflect on your vision and adjust your path.
- Stay aligned with your core values as your life expands.

Example:

- Early career → Focus on financial growth.
- Later career → Focus on creating impact and contribution.

Growth requires clarity — and clarity requires reflection.

2. Commit to Lifelong Learning

You will never "arrive."

- Keep learning.
- Keep expanding your skillset.
- Keep evolving your mindset.

Example:

- Attend conferences.

- Read new books.
- Surround yourself with people who challenge you.

Mastery requires a student's mindset.

3. Keep Strengthening Emotional Resilience

Life will continue to challenge you — but you'll get stronger with every test.

- Develop stress management tools.
- Strengthen your support system.
- Learn how to self-regulate under pressure.

Emotional strength creates long-term consistency.

4. Stay Connected to a Support System

Mindset mastery isn't a solo journey.

- Stay connected to coaches, mentors, and peers.
- Build new relationships as your life expands.
- Seek guidance and accountability when you need it.

Success accelerates through collective strength.

5. Stay Focused on Impact

Growth feels empty if you're only growing for yourself.

- Keep contributing.
- Keep lifting others.
- Keep creating opportunities for others to succeed.

True fulfillment comes from impact — not achievement.

Home Exercise: The Lifelong Mastery Plan

This exercise will help you stay grounded and focused on lifelong growth:

Step 1: Define Your Next Level of Growth

- What's the next version of you?
- What new challenges are you ready to face?

Step 2: Identify New Habits

- What daily actions will reinforce this new level of success?
- How can you adjust your strategy?

Step 3: Build a Support System

- Who will hold you accountable at the next level?
- Who will you learn from?

Step 4: Define Your Impact Goal

- How will you give back at this new level?
- What kind of legacy do you want to leave?

You've Already Won

You've built the mindset.
You've built the habits.
You've faced the challenges.
You've grown — and you've already succeeded.

Now it's about keeping the momentum going.

- Keep evolving.

- Keep expanding.
- Keep empowering.

Because success isn't a destination — it's who you are.

Mindset isn't what you know —
it's what you believe when no
one is watching.

Recap of Part 4:
Living the Empowered Life

Congratulations — you've completed *Part 4* of *Mindset Matters*!

Part 1 helped you build the foundation of a growth mindset.
Part 2 taught you how to regulate your emotions and develop consistency.
Part 3 guided you toward aligned action, confidence, and strategy.

But **Part 4** was where you stepped into your highest self.

This was the shift from **internal growth** to **external success**. From mastering your thoughts and emotions to creating a life that reflects your highest potential. You stopped working on your mindset — and started living it.

Part 4 was about **embodiment** — becoming the kind of person who naturally creates success, strength, and confidence in every area of life. It was about turning success from something you achieve into something you are.

Let's take a moment to reflect on what you've learned and how all the pieces come together:

Key Takeaways from Part 4

1. From Mindset to Lifestyle

- Mindset is the starting point — but consistency turns it into a lifestyle.
- When you align your identity, beliefs, and daily habits, success becomes effortless.
- You no longer rely on motivation — your habits and identity drive you automatically.

Example:

- Mindset → "I want to be healthy."
- Identity → "I am a healthy person."
- Lifestyle → Daily exercise, balanced meals, and mindfulness.

You stopped "trying" to succeed — you became the kind of person who naturally succeeds.

2. Navigating Challenges With Strength

- Setbacks and failures are inevitable — but they don't define you.
- Emotional agility allows you to handle challenges without losing momentum.
- You've learned how to separate emotion from action — and respond with strength and strategy.

Example:

- Business deal falls through → You adjust the strategy and try again.
- A personal conflict arises → You listen, regulate your emotions, and respond thoughtfully.

You've stopped fearing challenges — because you trust yourself to handle them.

3. Leaving a Legacy

   - True success isn't about personal accomplishment — it's about contribution.
   - Your greatest impact will come from helping others rise.
   - Legacy isn't about what you accumulate — it's about what you pass on.

Example:

- Mentoring a younger entrepreneur.
- Helping a friend rebuild confidence after a setback.
- Creating opportunities for others to succeed.

Success became meaningful when you started giving back.

4. The Lifelong Journey of Mindset Mastery

   - Mindset mastery is not a destination — it's a lifelong process of growth and expansion.
   - Your goals and vision will evolve as you grow — and you now have the tools to adapt and expand with them.
   - You've learned how to stay grounded, motivated, and confident through every phase of life.

Example:

- Business growth → Adjust your strategy as you scale.
- Personal growth → Expand your definition of success.
- Life changes → Stay grounded and aligned through transitions.

You've built a foundation that will serve you for life — no matter what comes next.

How It All Fits Together

You've now completed the full cycle of mindset mastery:

1. **Mindset** → Shifted from fixed to growth.
2. **Emotional Regulation** → Mastered emotional control and resilience.
3. **Clarity** → Defined your vision and aligned your identity.
4. **Consistency** → Built momentum through daily action.
5. **Challenge Management** → Learned how to face setbacks with strength.
6. **Contribution** → Stepped into leadership and legacy.

This is the cycle that drives lifelong growth — every time you reach a new level, you will return to these same principles to level up again.

You've built a mental framework that will allow you to succeed in any situation — not because life will get easier, but because **you've become stronger.**

Home Exercise: The Empowered Life Blueprint

This exercise will help you apply everything you've learned and create a framework for ongoing success and fulfillment.

Step 1: Define Your Identity at This Level

- Who are you now that you've completed this journey?
- What kind of person creates the success you desire?

Example:

- *"I am a confident and disciplined business leader."*
- *"I am a grounded and loving partner."*
- *"I am a resilient and healthy person."*

Step 2: Identify 3 Core Habits That Will Sustain This Identity

- What daily actions will reinforce this identity?
- What habits will help you maintain consistency and momentum?

Example:
Morning journaling to maintain clarity.
Daily outreach to grow your business.
Weekly reflection to stay grounded.

Step 3: Create a Support System

- Who will hold you accountable at this level?
- Who will you learn from?
- How will you stay connected to people who elevate you?

Example:
Join a mastermind group for business growth.

Partner with a coach for strategic advice.
Build a personal support system for emotional resilience.

Step 4: Define Your Contribution Goal

- How will you give back at this new level of success?
- What kind of legacy do you want to create?

Example:
Mentor three young entrepreneurs.
Share your story publicly to inspire others.
Donate time and resources to causes aligned with your values.

Step 5: Reflect and Adjust Monthly

- Growth is a lifelong process — check in with yourself regularly.
- What's working?
- What needs to be adjusted?

Example:
Monthly journaling session.
Feedback session with a mentor.
Progress check on key goals.

Group Exercise: Empowerment Mastermind

This exercise works even better with a group:

1. Pair up or work in small groups.
2. Share your identity statement and core habits.
3. Give each other feedback and suggestions.
4. Agree to hold each other accountable.
5. Check in weekly or monthly.

Example:

- Business Mastermind → Check in on business strategy and growth.
- Fitness Group → Check in on workouts and health goals.
- Personal Growth Group → Share wins and struggles and offer encouragement.

You've Become the Person You Once Wished You Were

Think back to where you started — the version of you that picked up this book.

- You were curious, but unsure.
- Motivated, but inconsistent.
- Ready for growth but still doubting yourself.

That version of you no longer exists.

- You've built confidence and strength.
- You've learned how to regulate your emotions and respond with clarity.
- You've discovered how to create momentum through consistent action.
- You've learned how to rise after failure.
- You've started creating impact through contribution.

You've BECOME the person you once looked up to.

And now — it's about continuing to grow and expand from this foundation.

Final Thought:

"Mindset mastery isn't about becoming someone new — it's about becoming the fullest version of yourself."

You've already won — now it's about living that victory.

Go build your future.
Go rise after setbacks.
Go create impact.
Go claim the life you were born for.

Because you are ready — and you've always been enough.

You are empowered. You are capable. You are limitless.

Now go live like it.

Stay Connected with Dr. Shamarah J. Hutchins
TheMindologist | CEO of Serene Corporation

Thank you for journeying through Mindset Matters. Your commitment to personal growth and transformation is commendable. Dr. Shamarah J. Hutchins, also known as TheMindologist, is dedicated to supporting individuals like you in cultivating a resilient mindset and achieving holistic well-being.

Online Presence
- Website: www.themindologistdoc.com

Social Media
- Instagram: @TheMindologist
- Facebook: @TheMindologist
- LinkedIn: Dr. Shamarah Thomas-Hutchins

Join the Community
Join HERSociety on Facebook!
@HERSocietybyHERology

Contact Information
Email: bookingthemindologist@gmail.com
Phone: 1-866-287-MIND (6463)

Stay empowered, and remember: Your mindset shapes your reality. Continue to cultivate it with intention.

www.ingramcontent.com/pod-product-compliance
Lightning Source LLC
Chambersburg PA
CBHW061736070526
44585CB00024B/2698